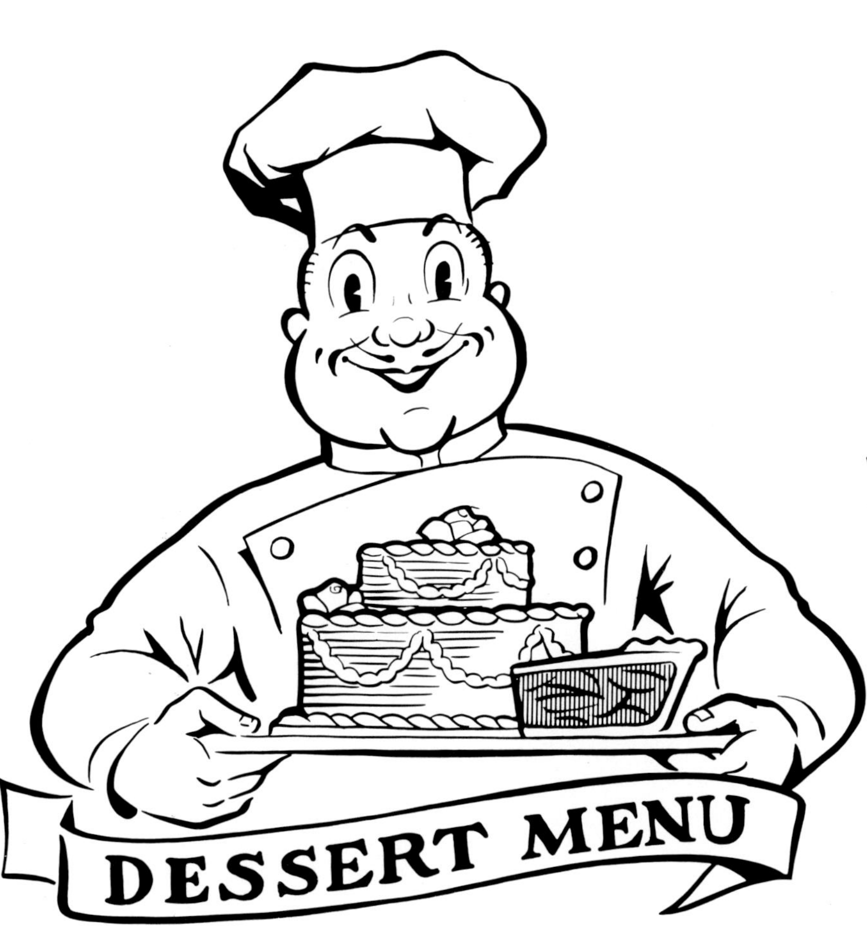
DESSERT MENU

DESSERT MENU

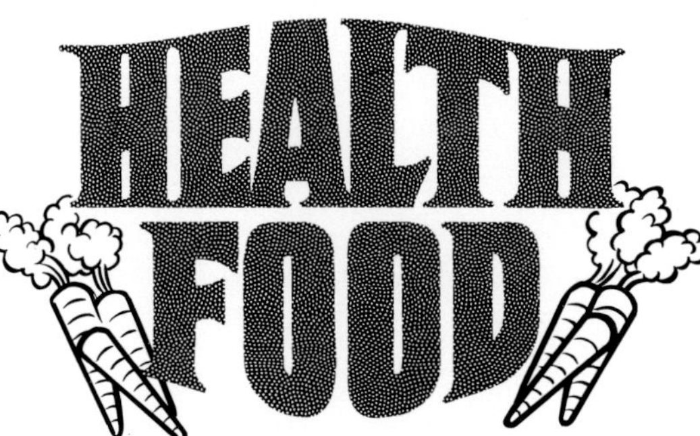
HEALTH
FOOD

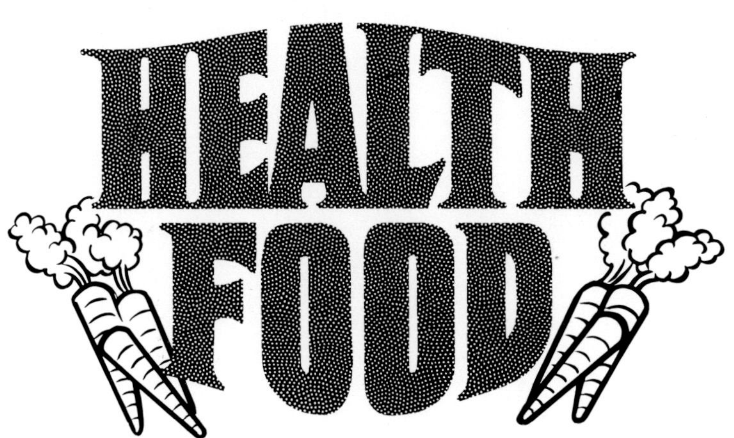
HEALTH
FOOD

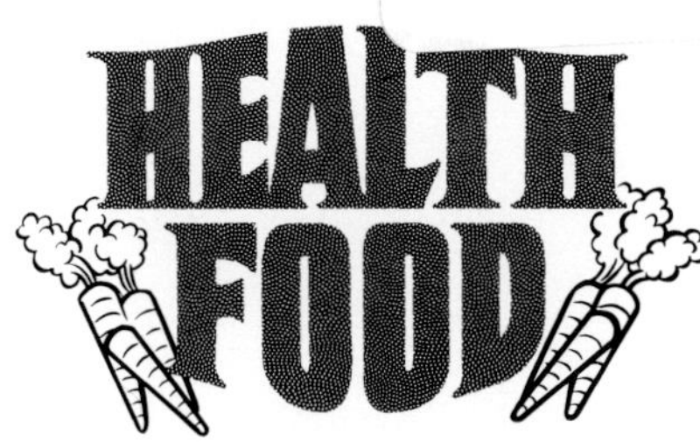
HEALTH
FOOD

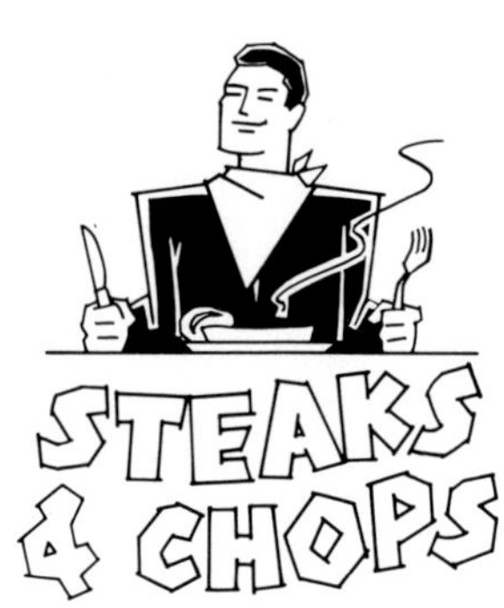
STEAKS
& CHOPS
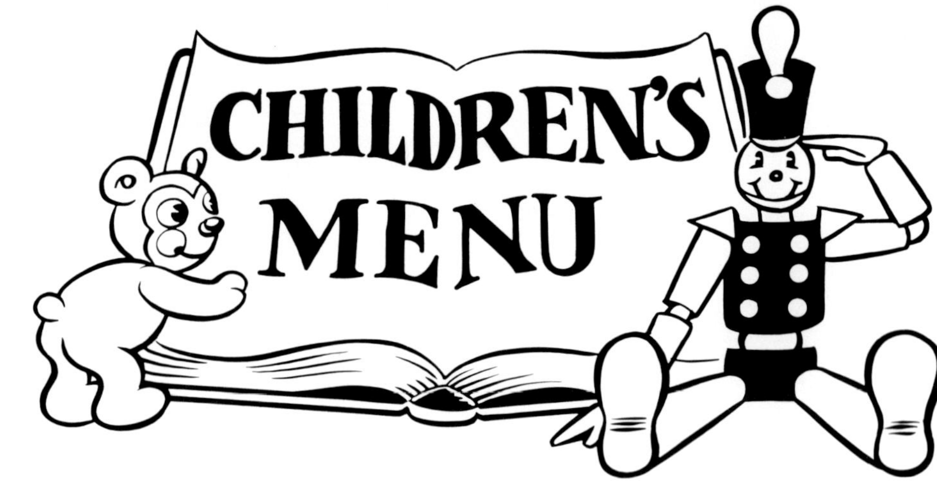
CHILDREN'S
MENU
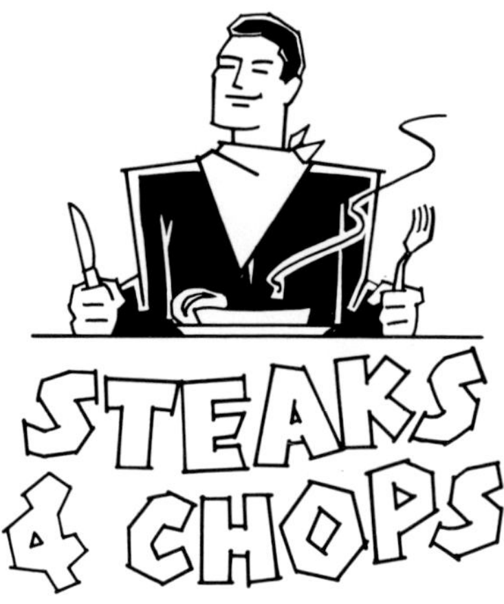
STEAKS
& CHOPS
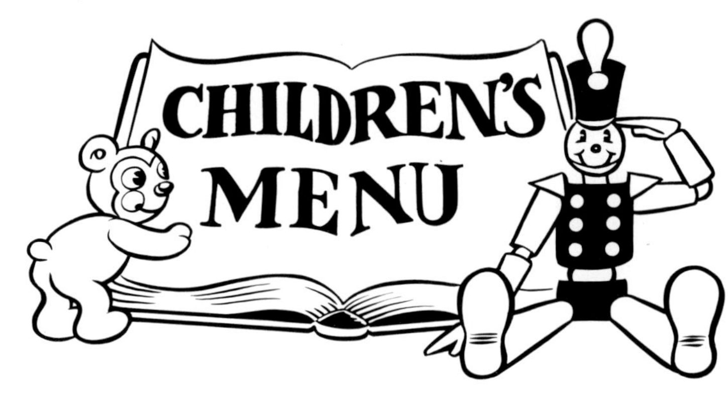
CHILDREN'S
MENU
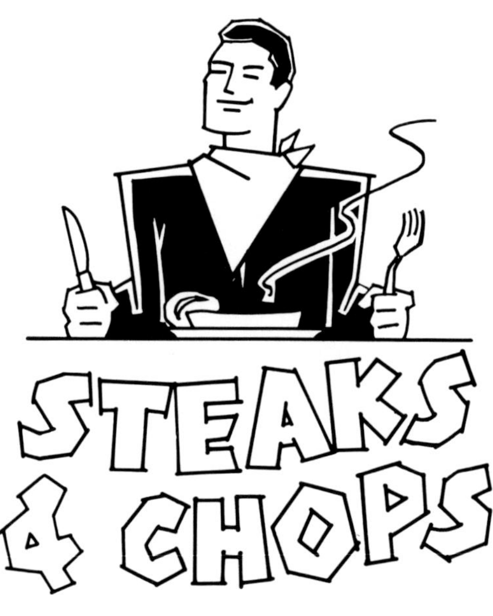
STEAKS
& CHOPS
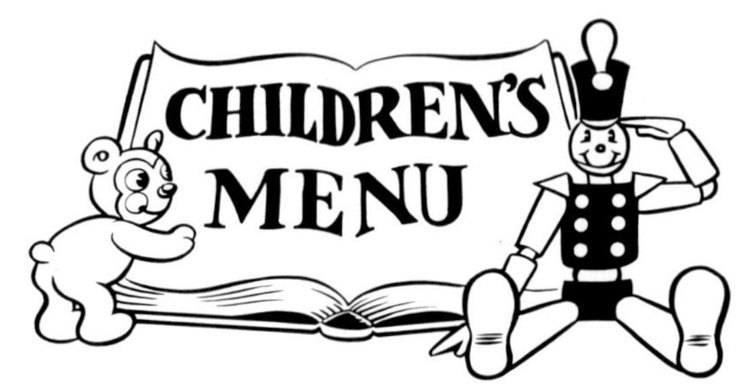
CHILDREN'S
MENU
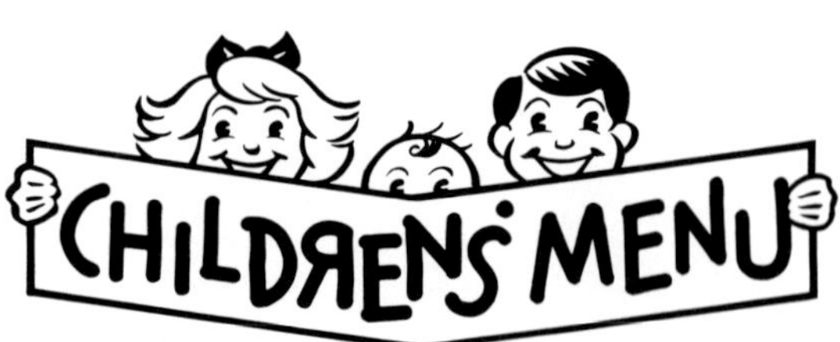
CHILDRENS' MENU
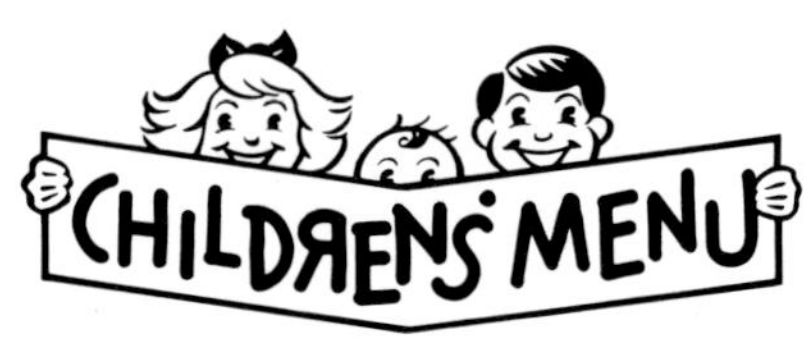
CHILDRENS' MENU
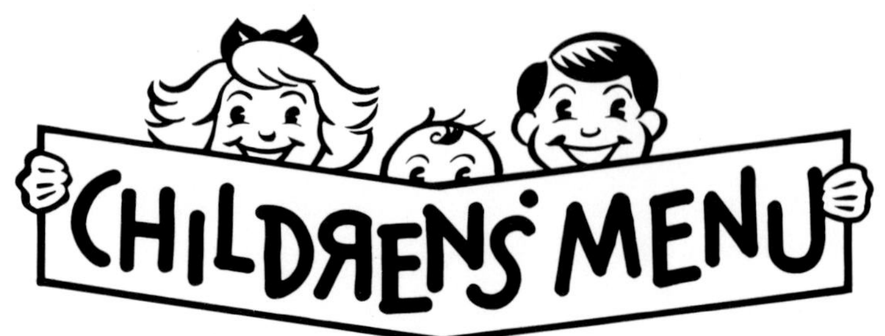
CHILDRENS' MENU

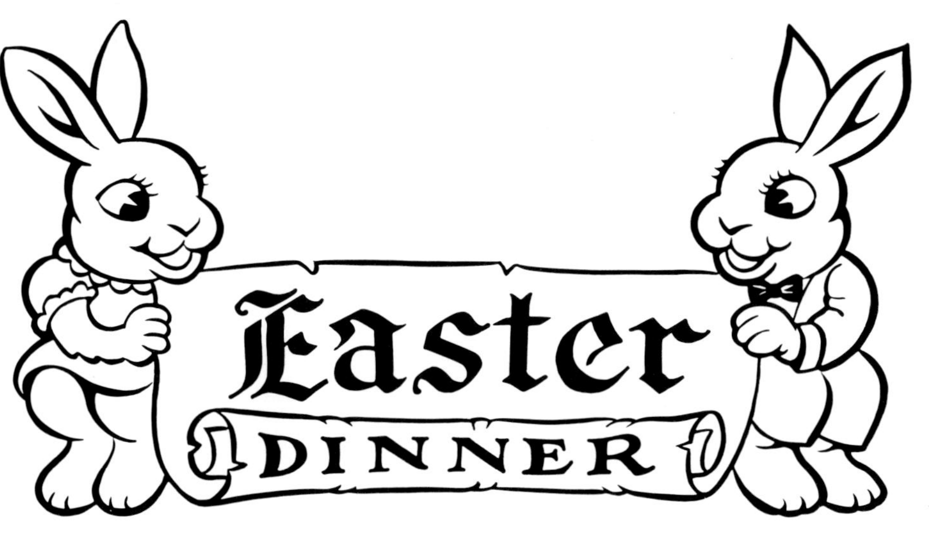
Easter
DINNER

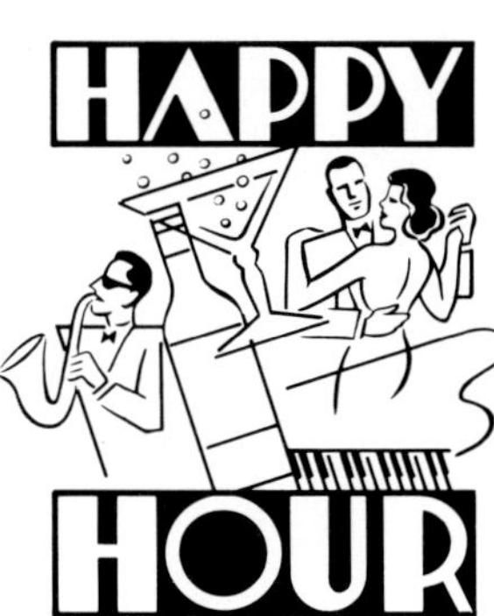
HAPPY
HOUR

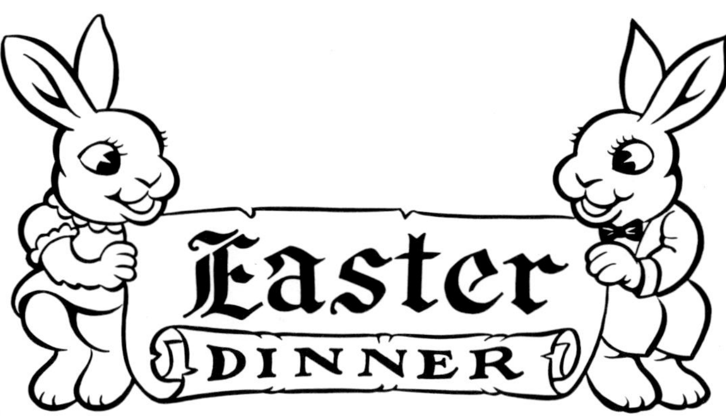
Easter
DINNER

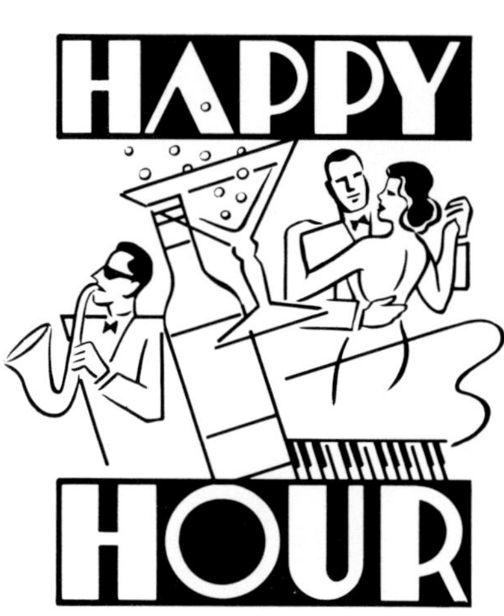
HAPPY
HOUR

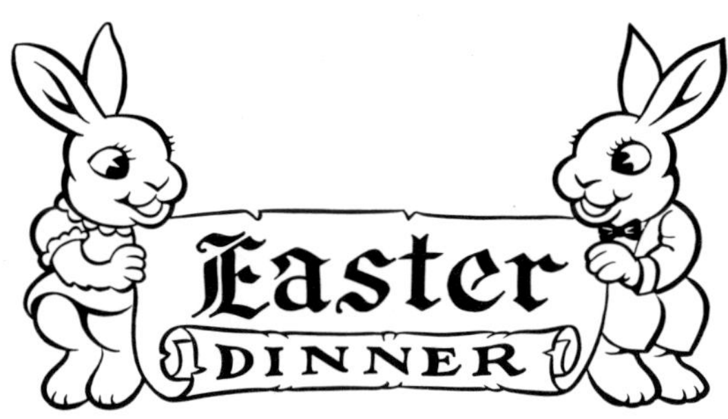
Easter
DINNER

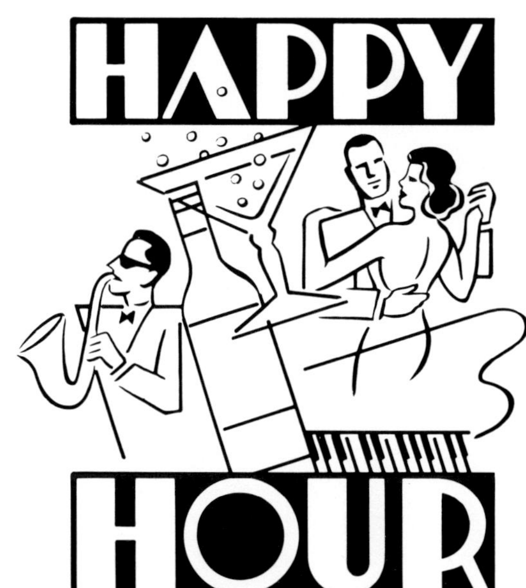
HAPPY
HOUR

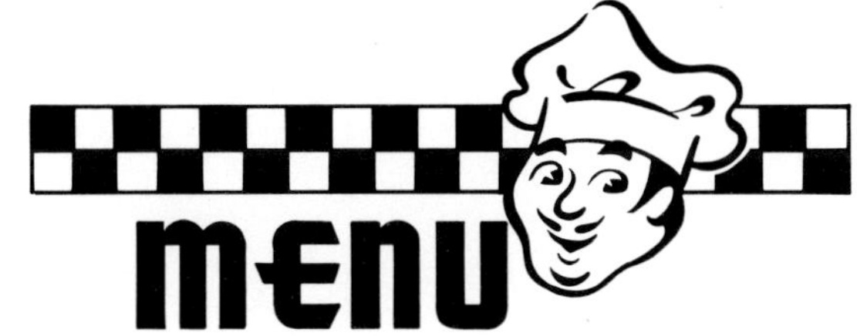
MENU

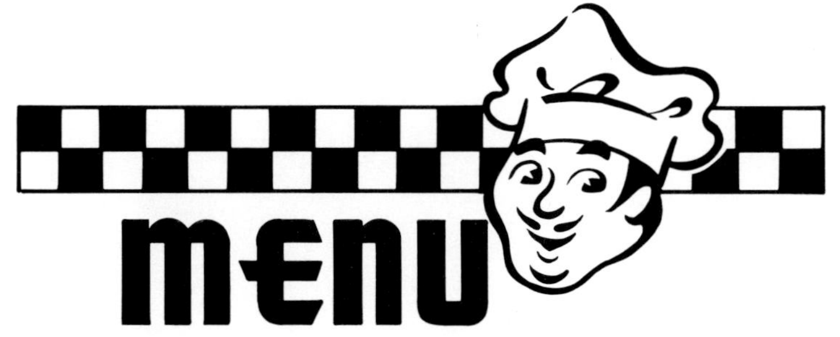
MENU

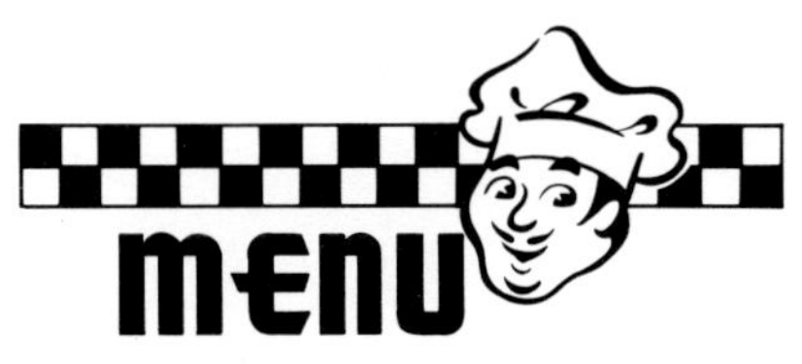
MENU

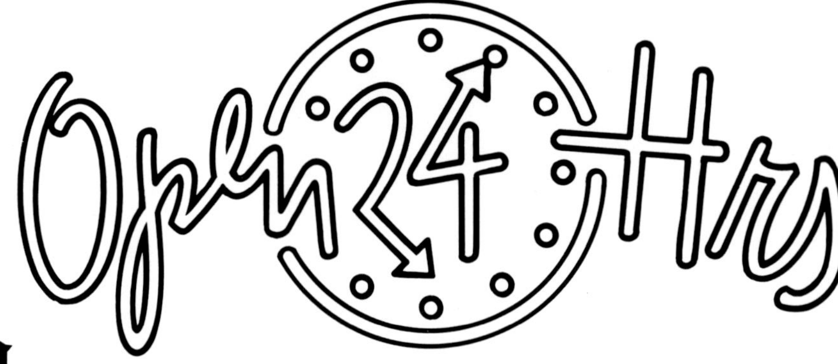
Open 24 Hrs

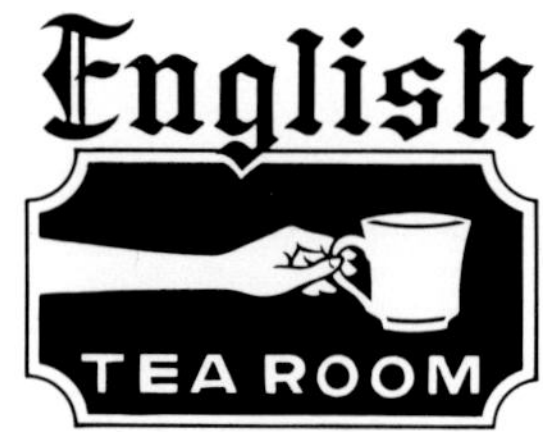
English
TEA ROOM

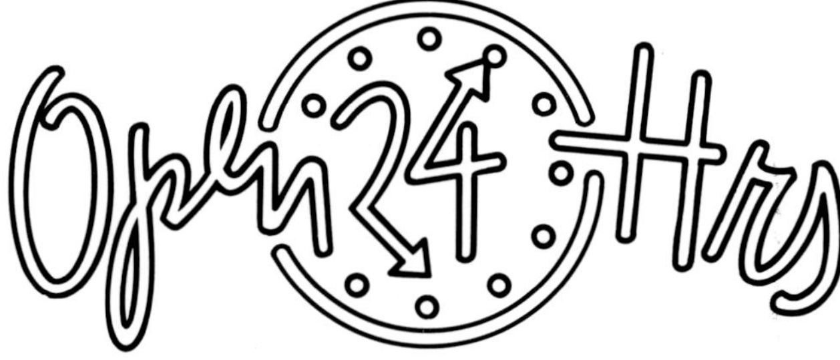
Open 24 Hrs

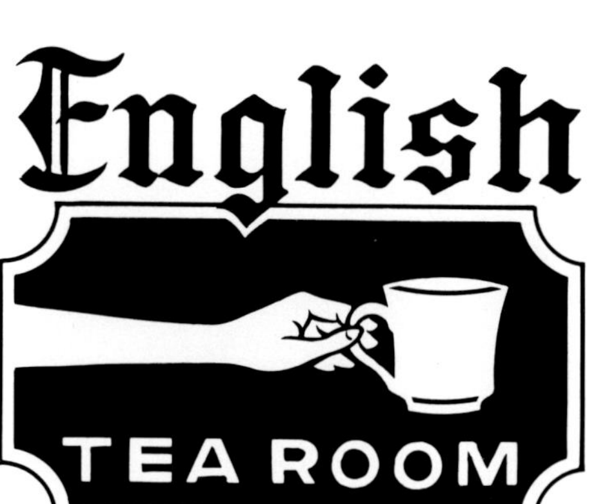
English
TEA ROOM

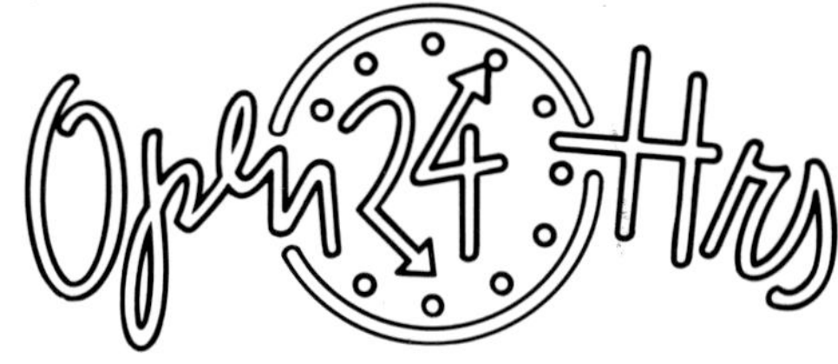
Open 24 Hrs

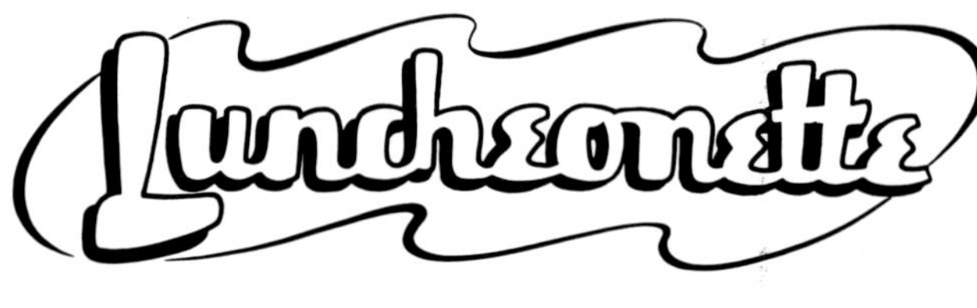
Luncheonette

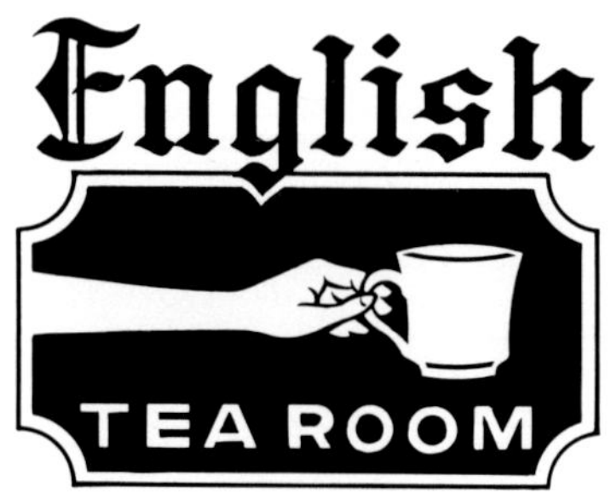
English
TEA ROOM

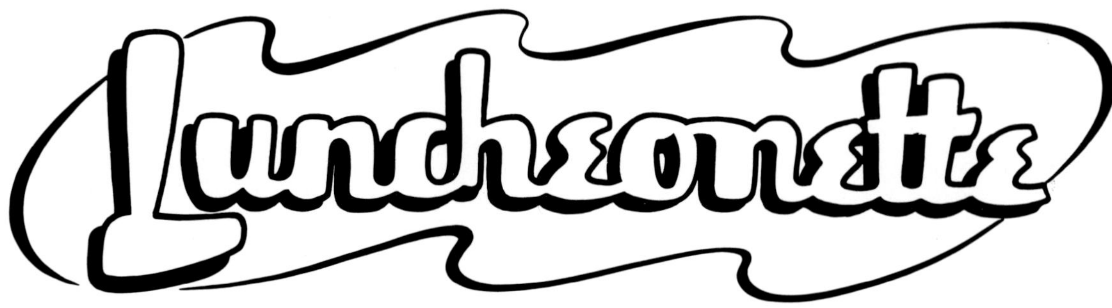
Luncheonette

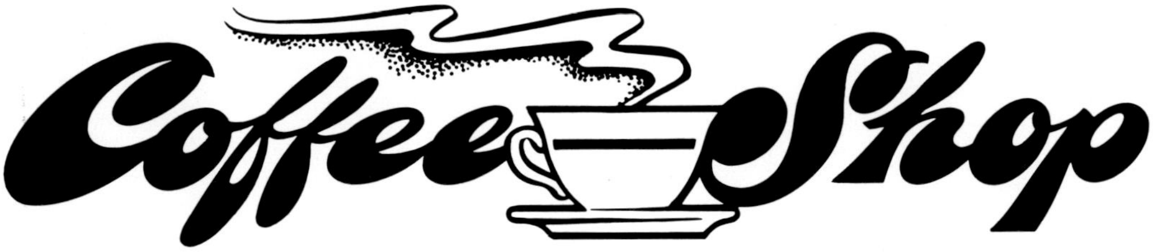

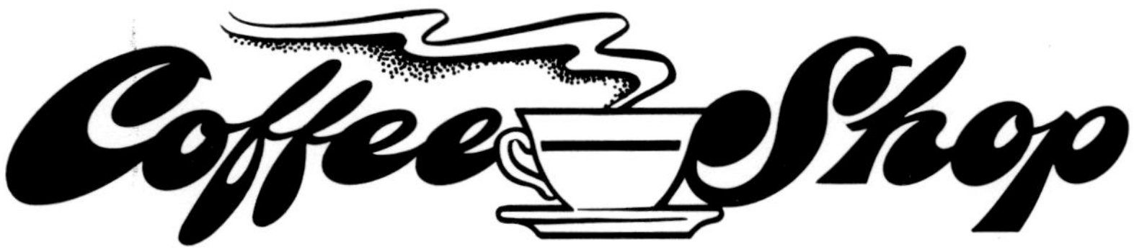

Coffee Shop

Coffee Shop

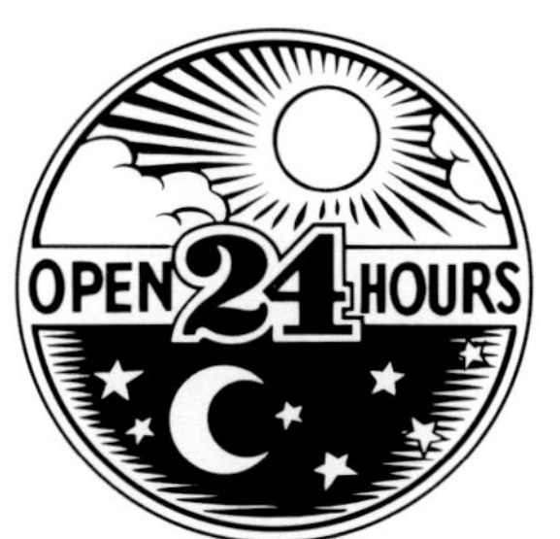

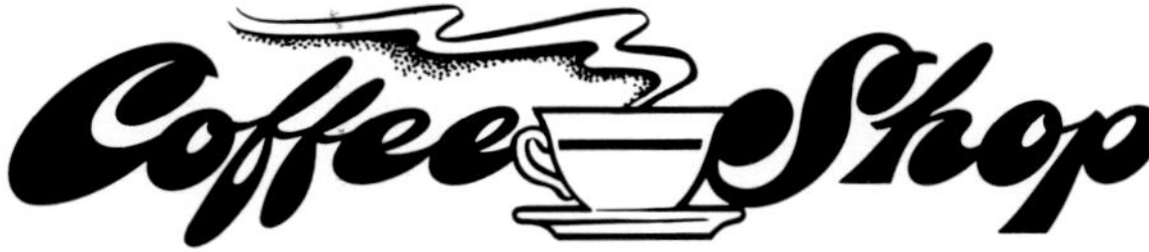

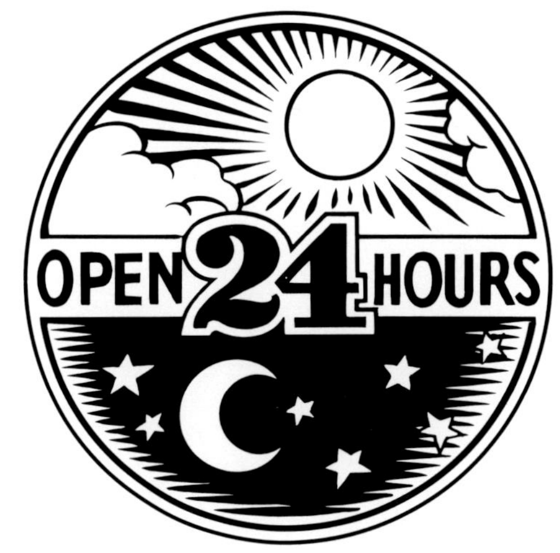

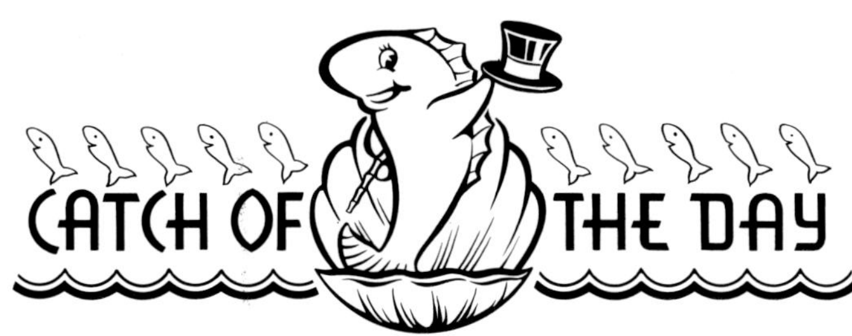

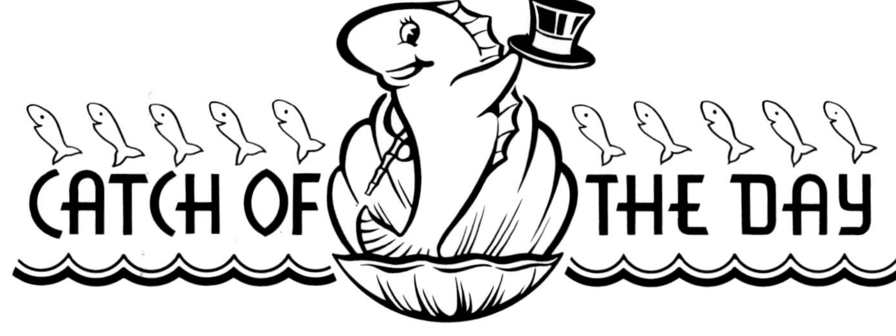

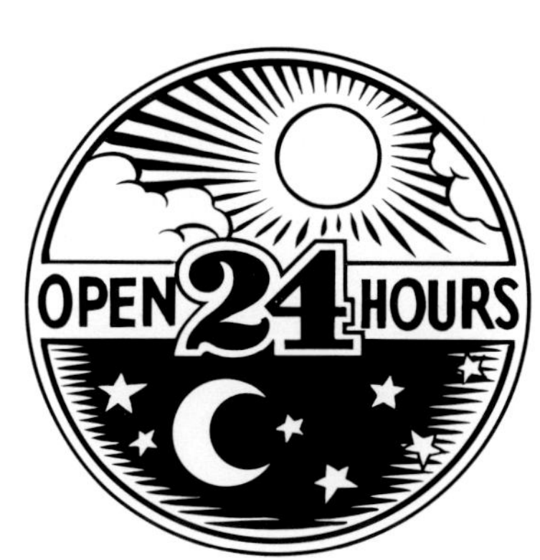

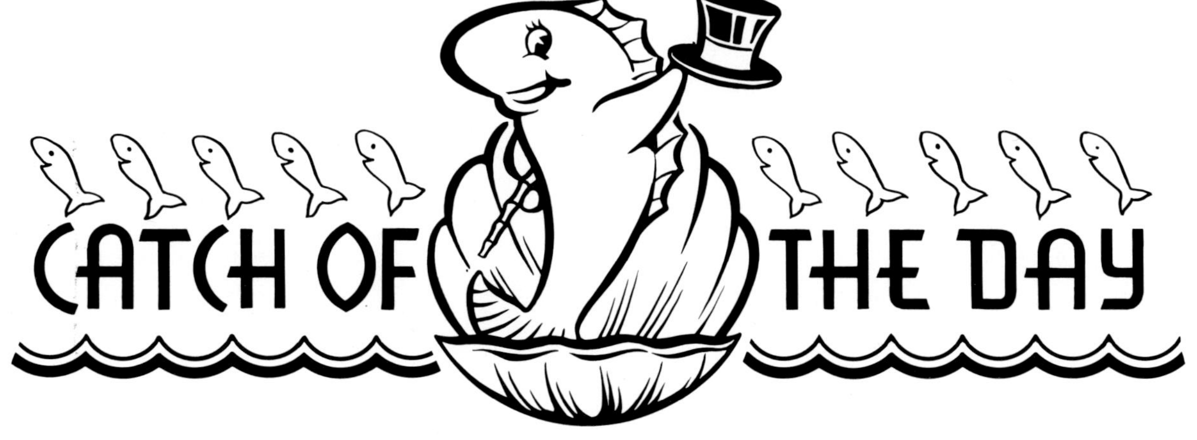

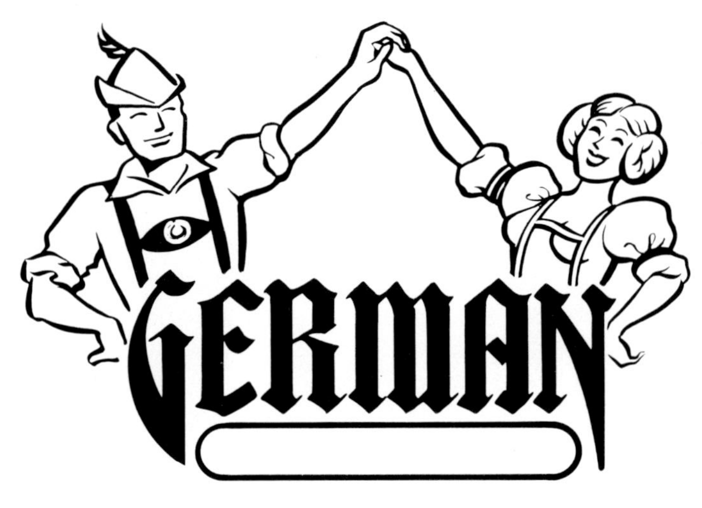
GERMAN
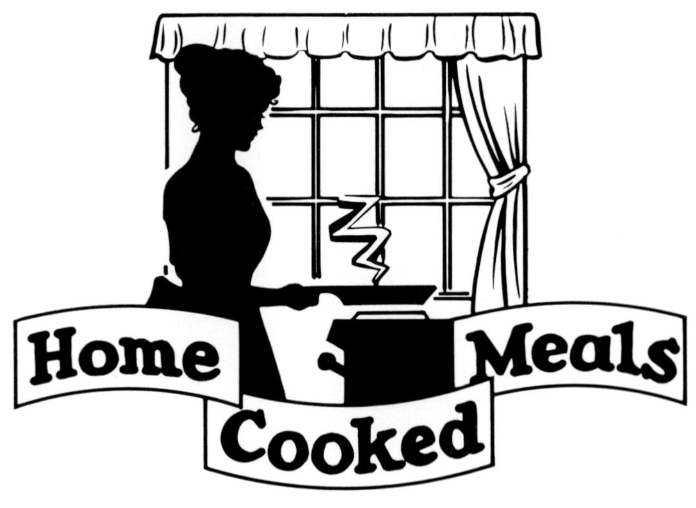
Home
Cooked
Meals
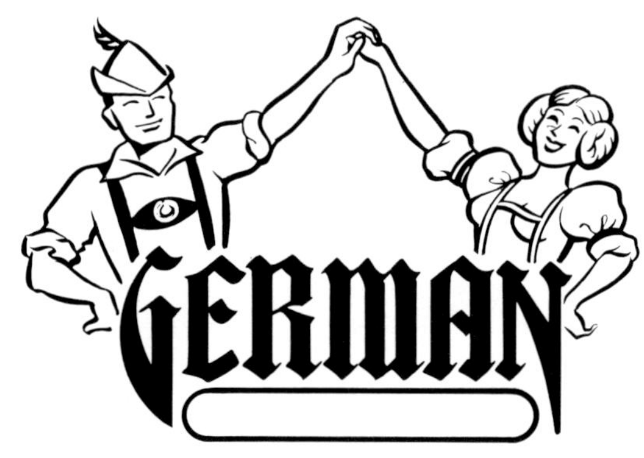
GERMAN
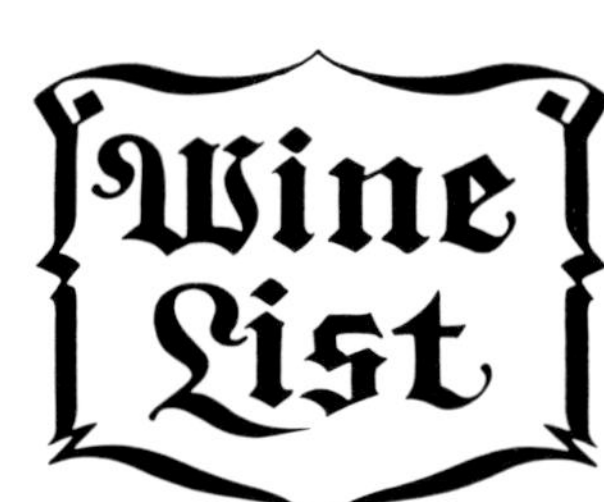
Wine
List
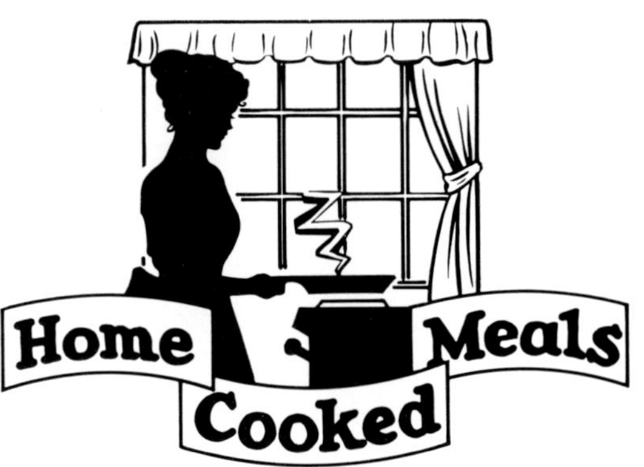
Home
Cooked
Meals
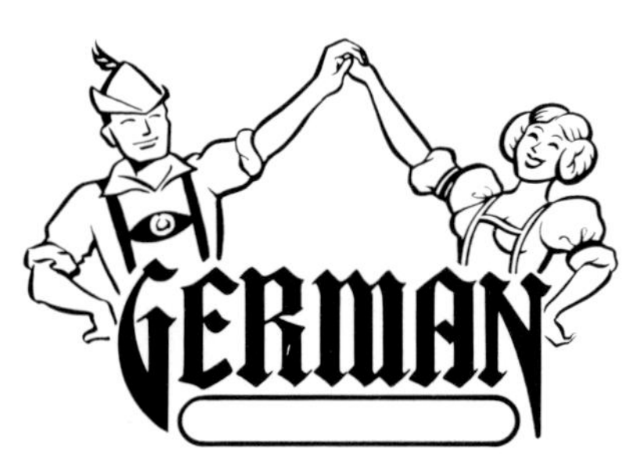
GERMAN
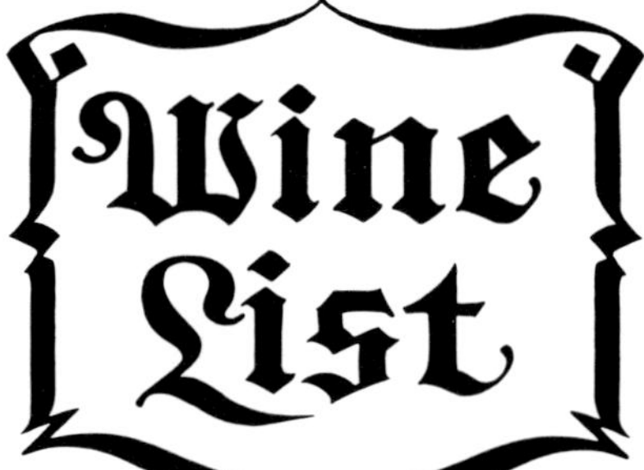
Wine
List
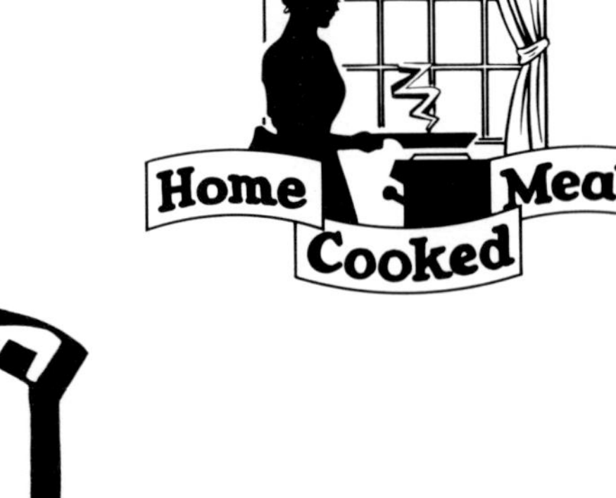
Home
Cooked
Meals
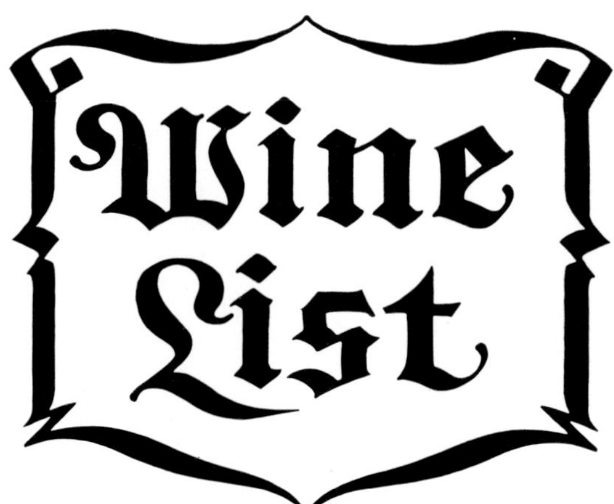
Wine
List

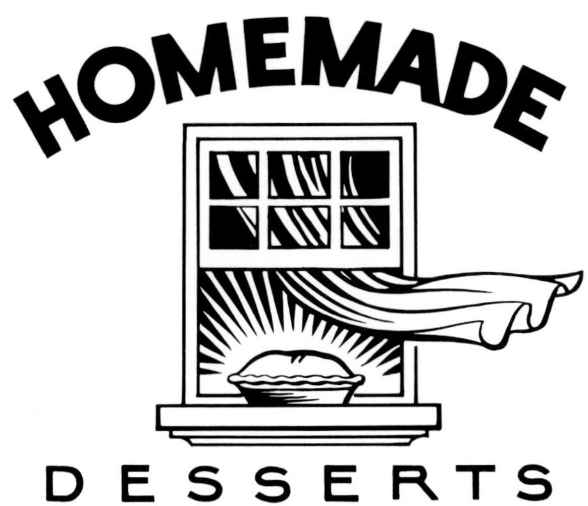
HOMEMADE
DESSERTS
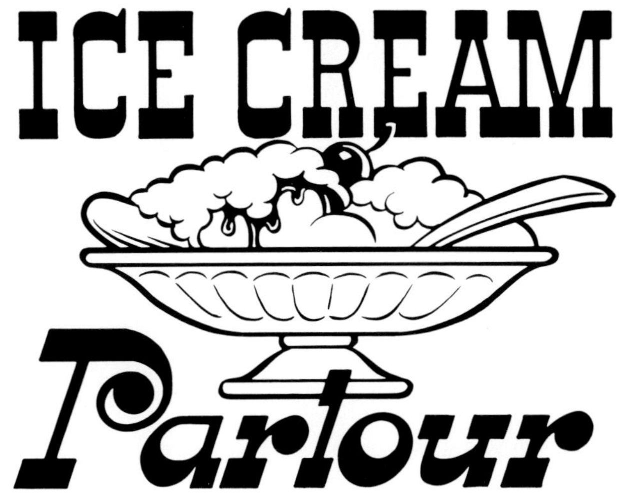
ICE CREAM
Parlour
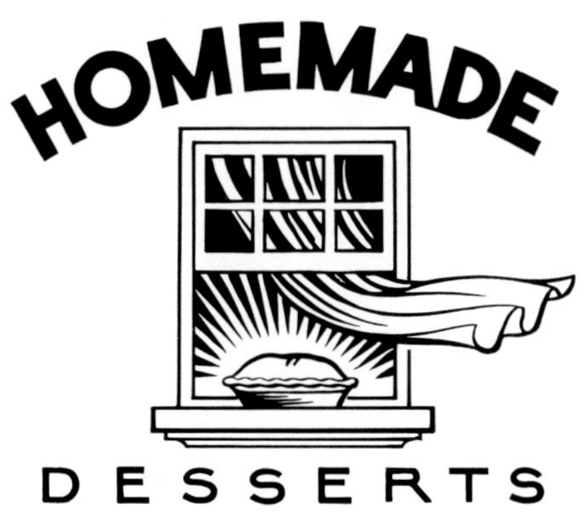
HOMEMADE
DESSERTS
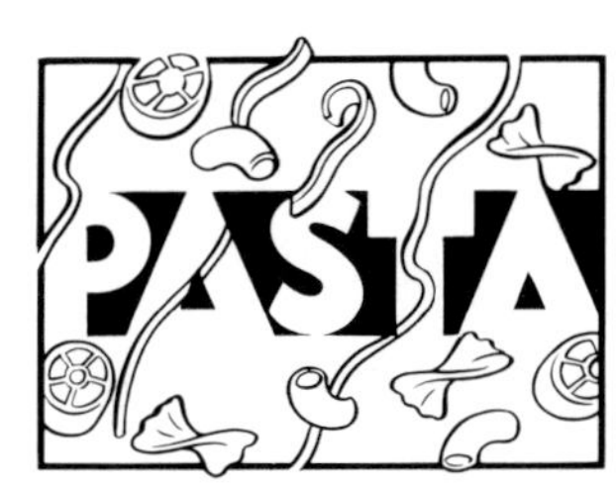
PASTA
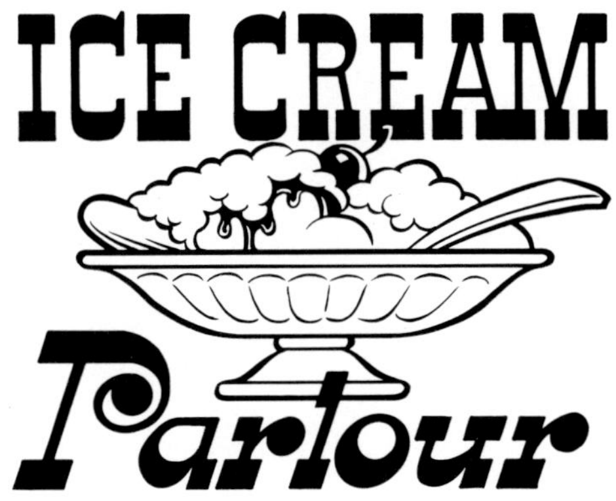
ICE CREAM
Parlour
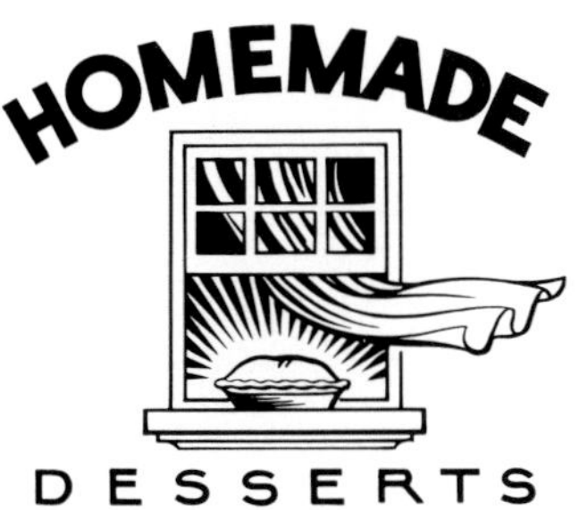
HOMEMADE
DESSERTS
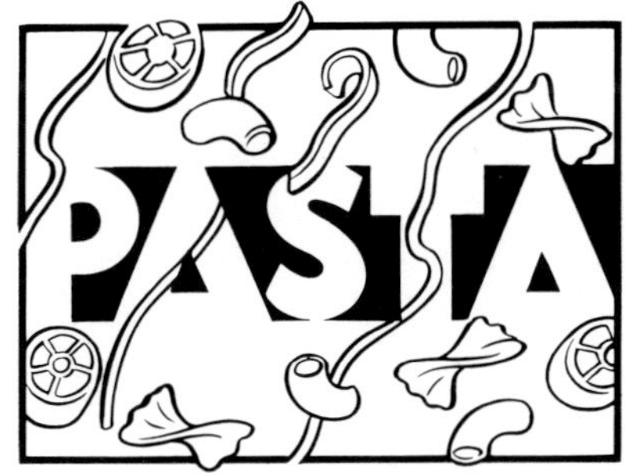
PASTA
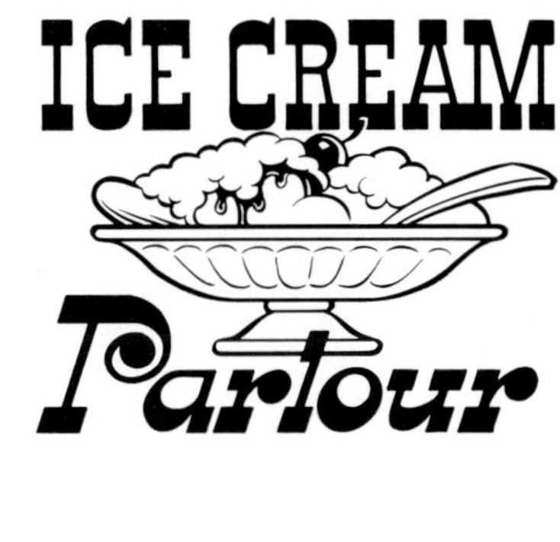
ICE CREAM
Parlour
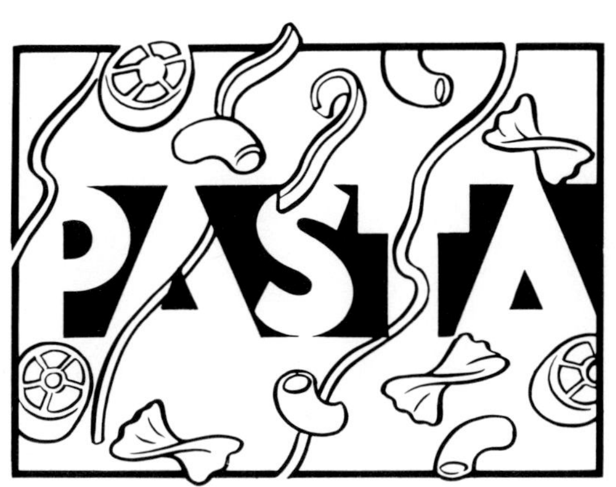
PASTA

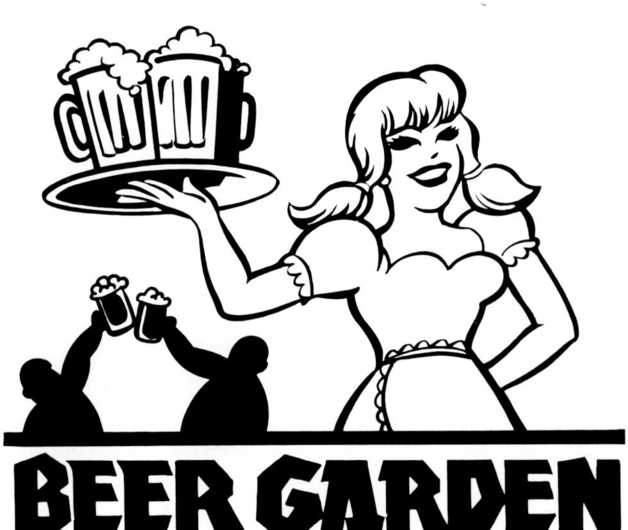
BEER GARDEN

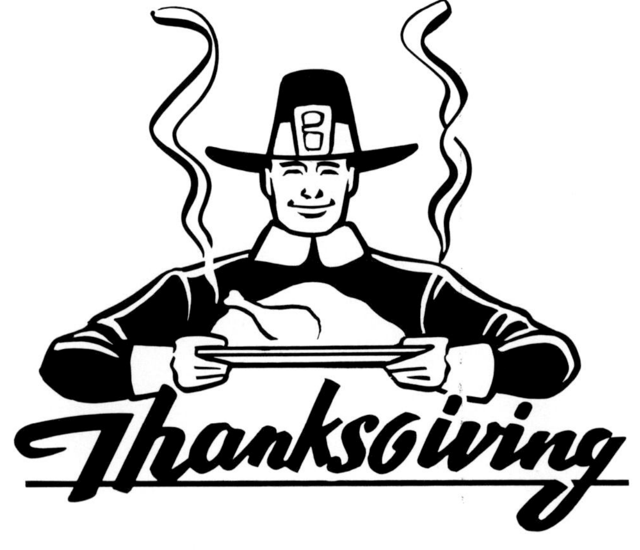
Thanksgiving

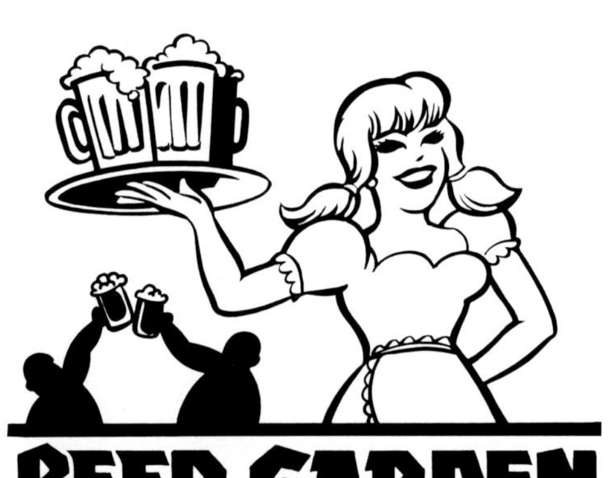

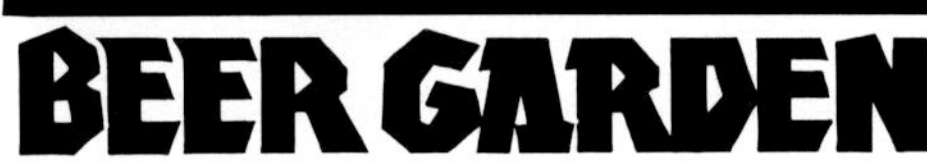
BEER GARDEN

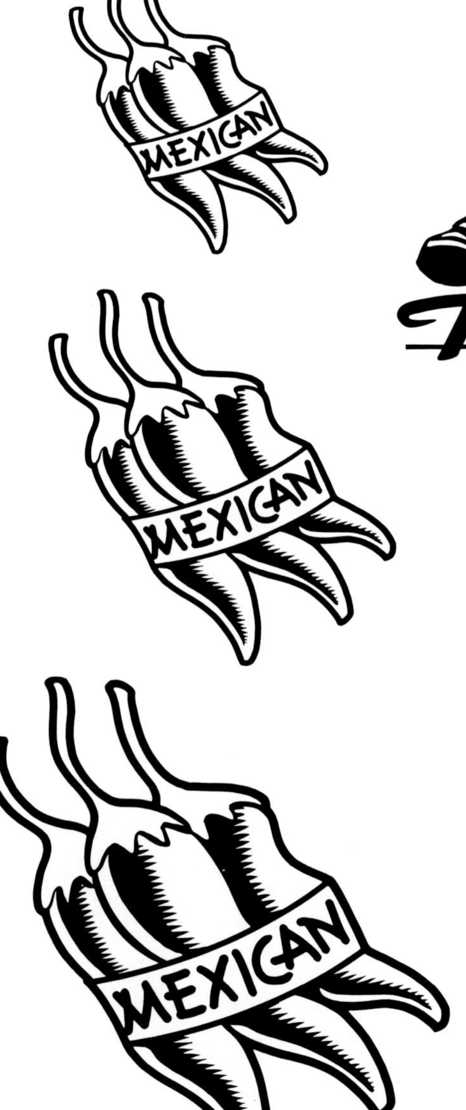
MEXICAN
MEXICAN
MEXICAN

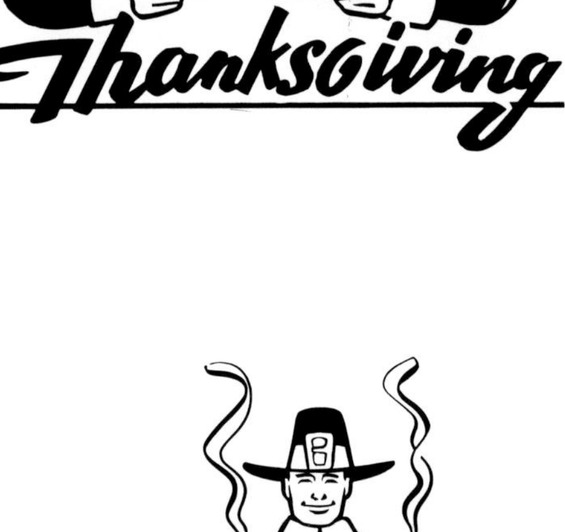
Thanksgiving

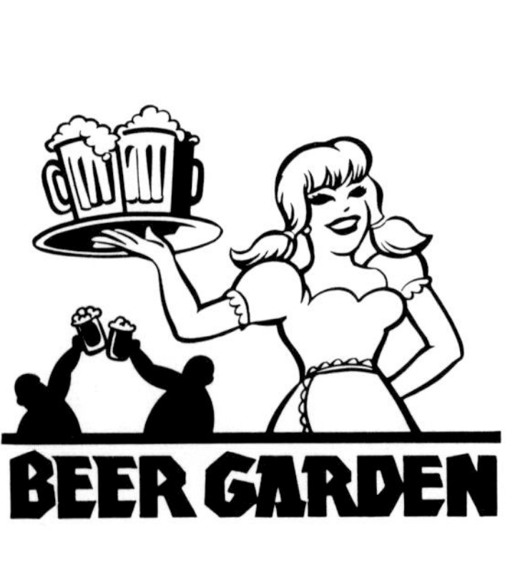
BEER GARDEN

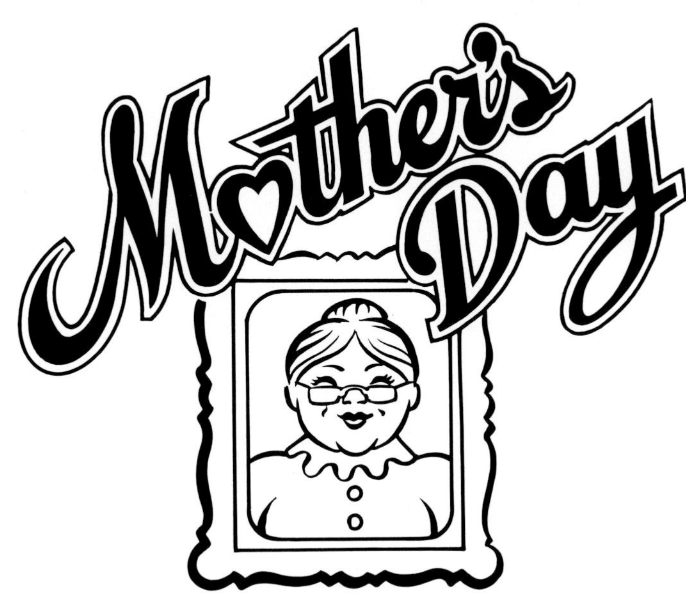
Mother's Day

CAKES

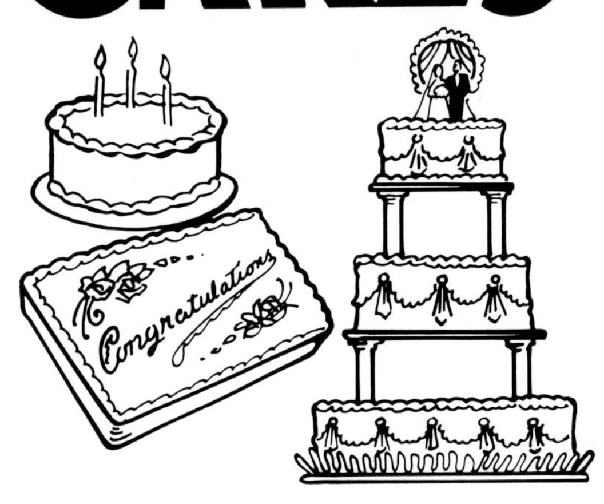
Congratulations

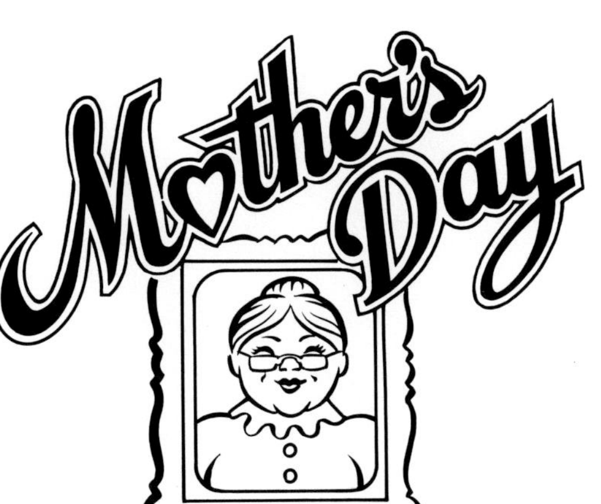
Mother's Day

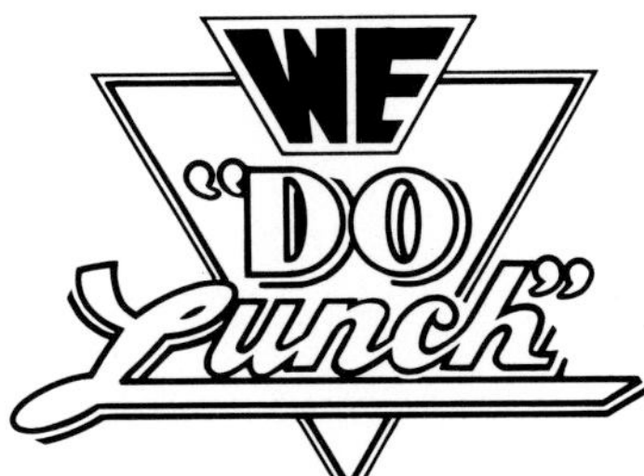
WE "DO Lunch"

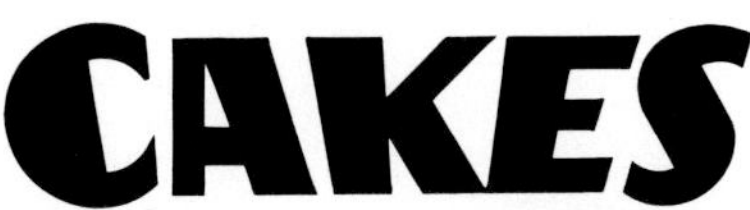
CAKES

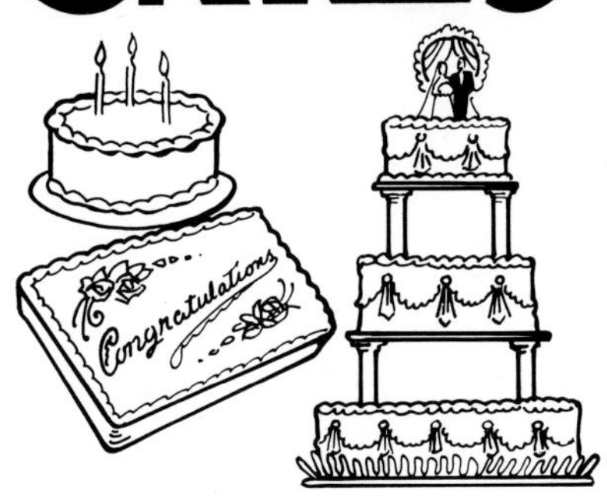
Congratulations

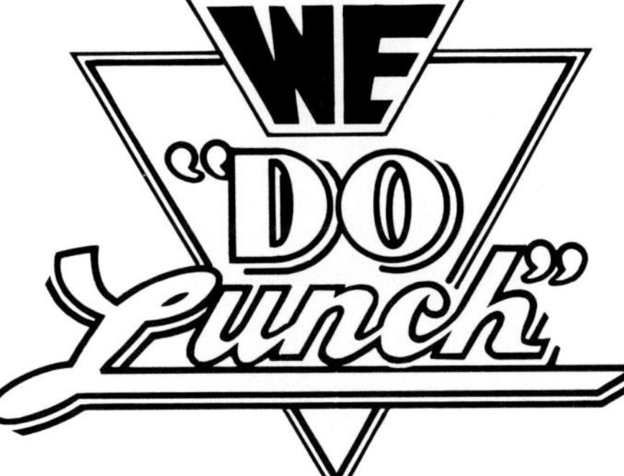
WE "DO Lunch"

CAKES

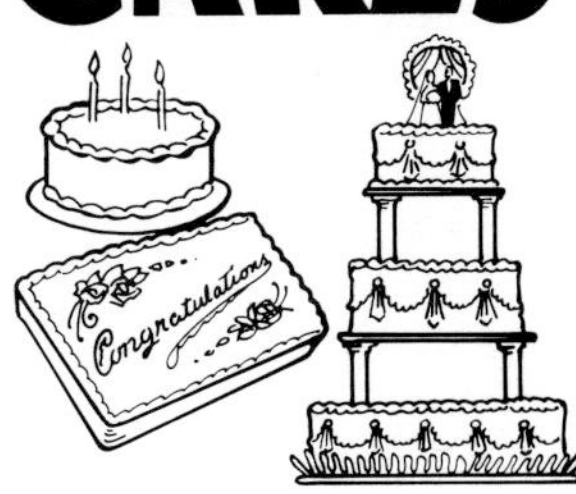
Congratulations

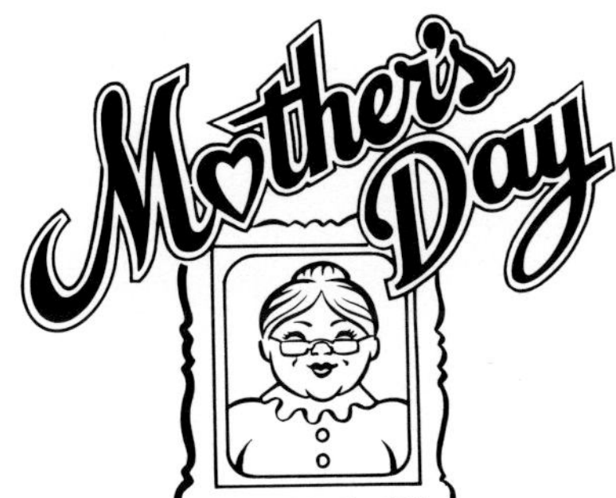
Mother's Day

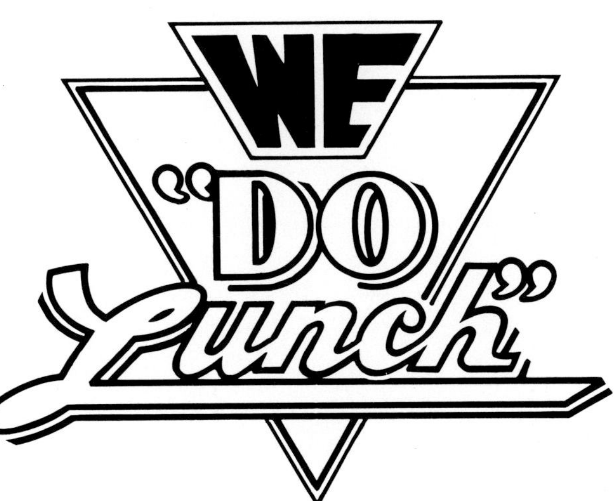
WE "DO Lunch"

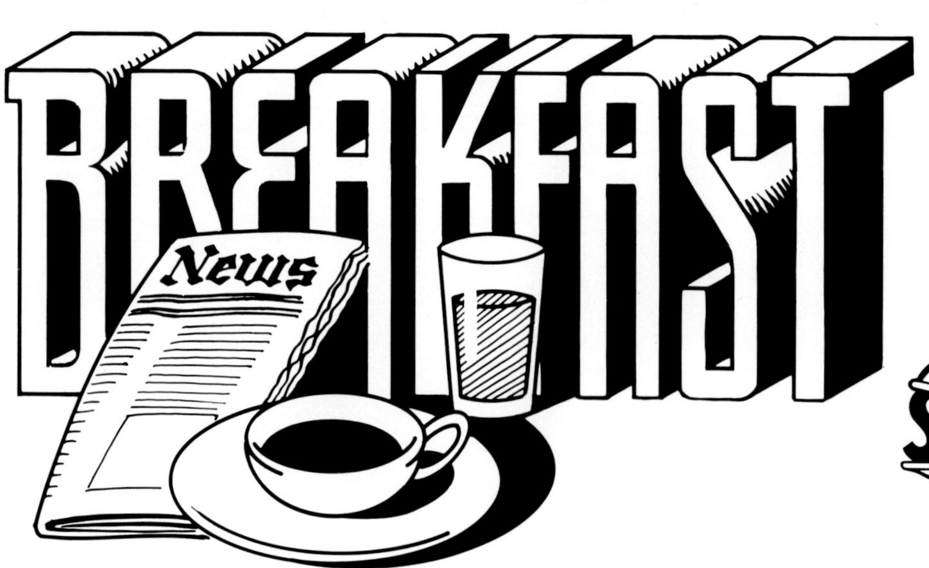
BREAKFAST
News

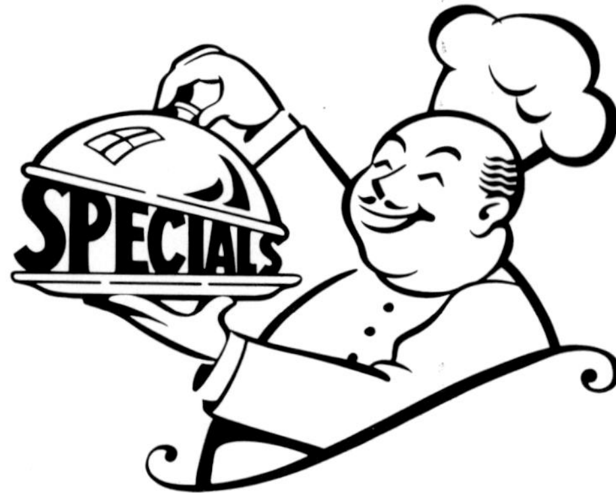
SPECIALS

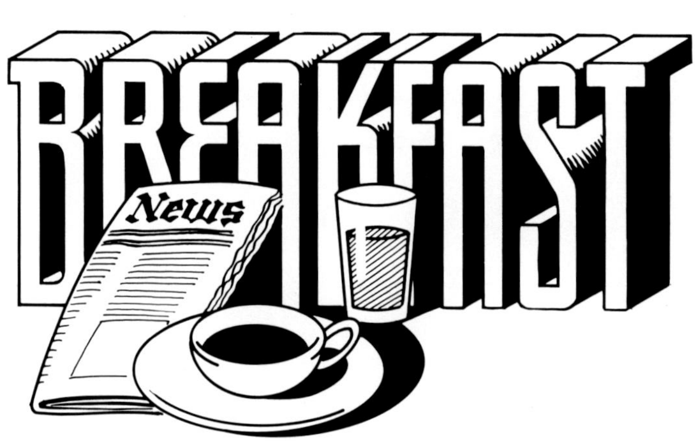
BREAKFAST
News

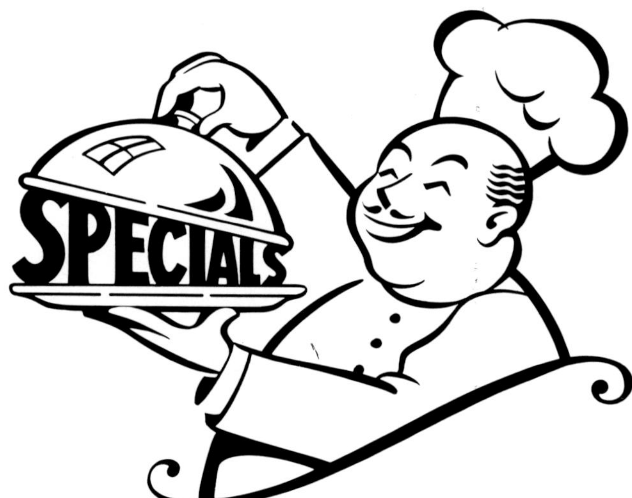
SPECIALS

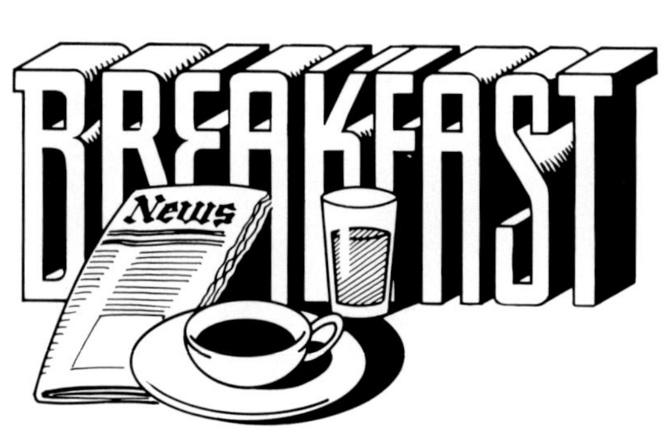
BREAKFAST
News

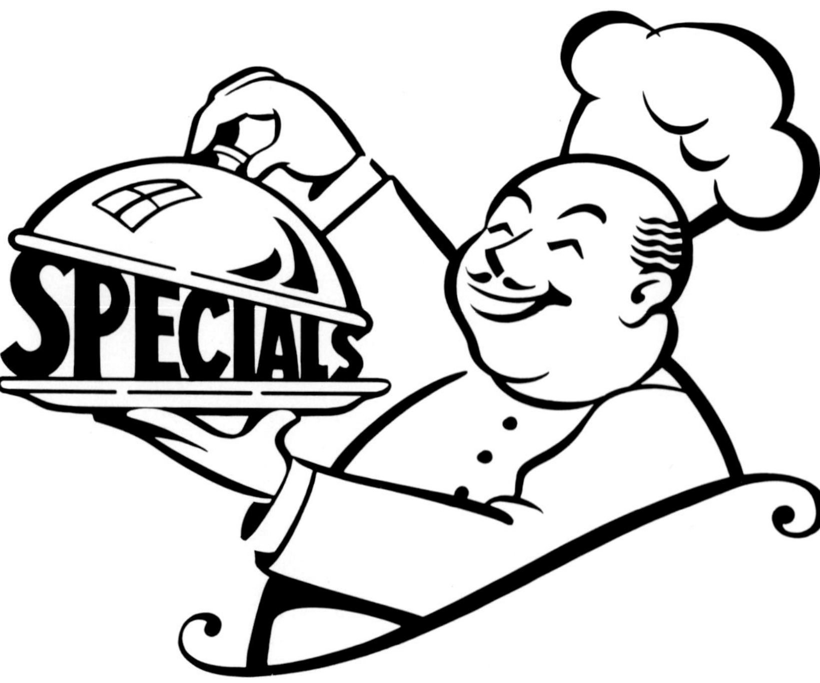
SPECIALS

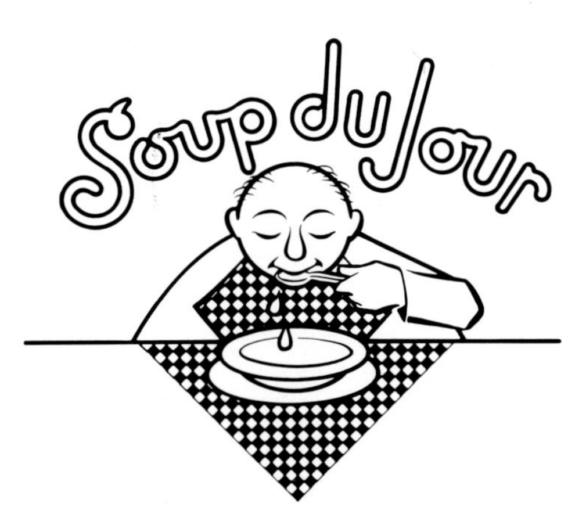
Soup du Jour

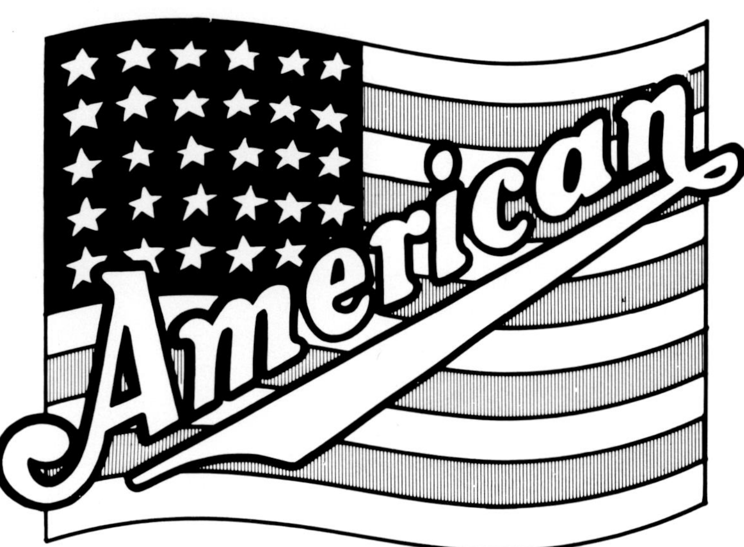
American

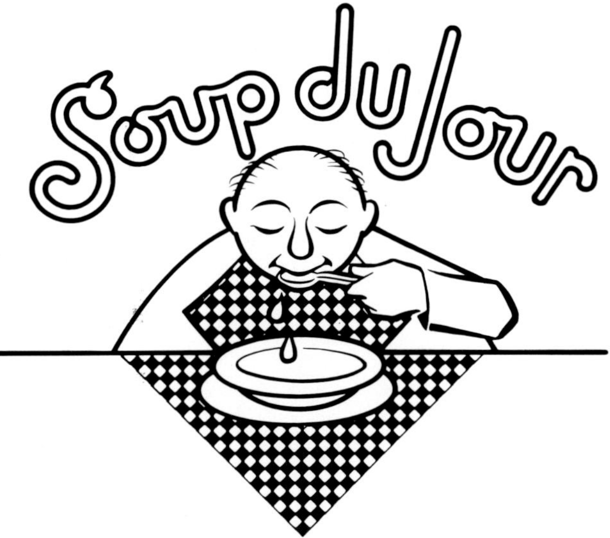
Soup du Jour

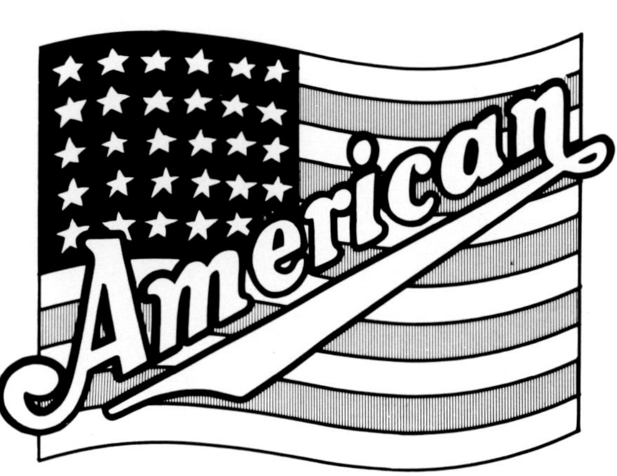
American

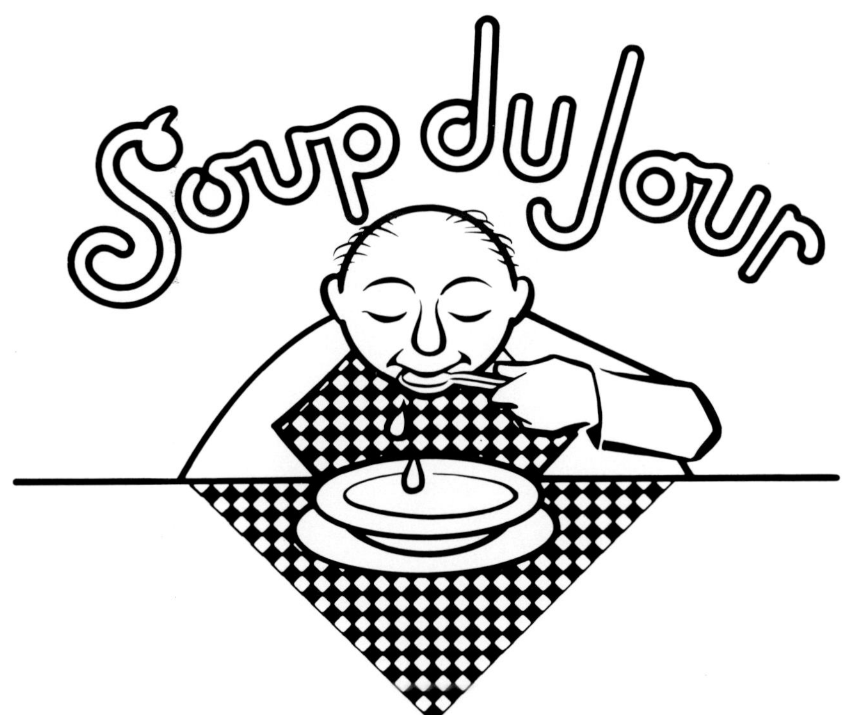
Soup du Jour

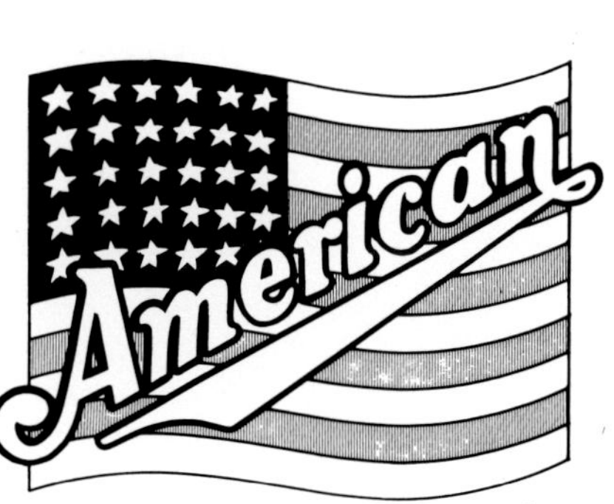
American

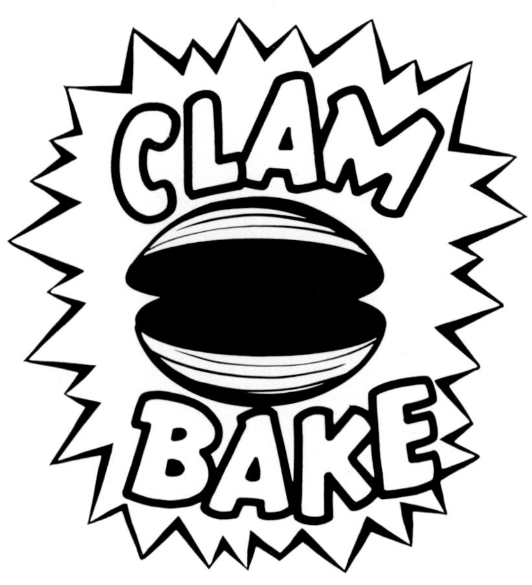
CLAM
BAKE

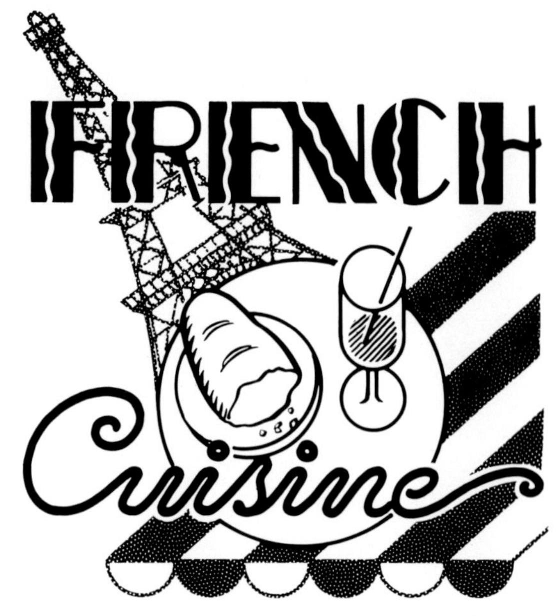
FRENCH
Cuisine

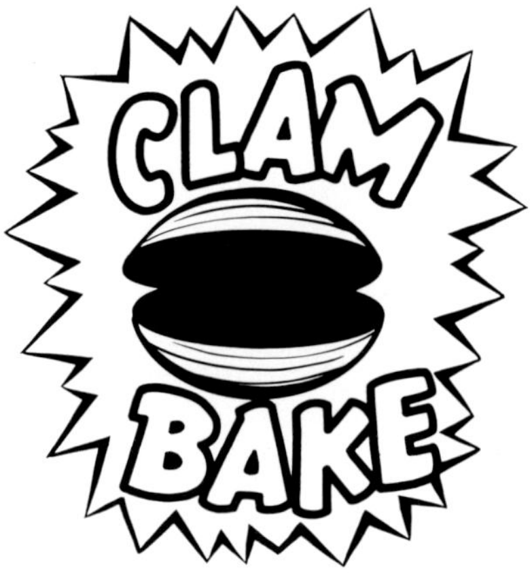

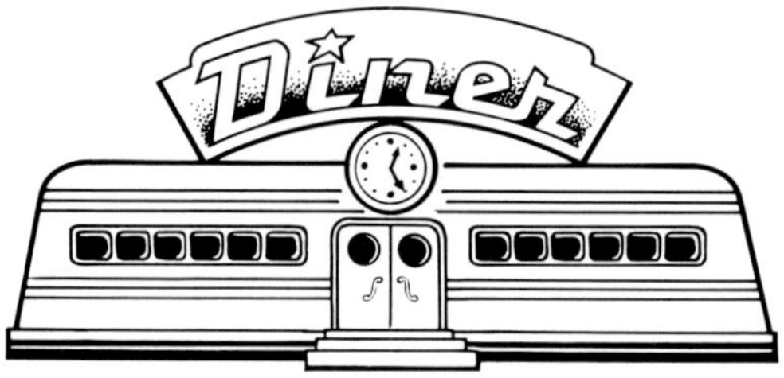

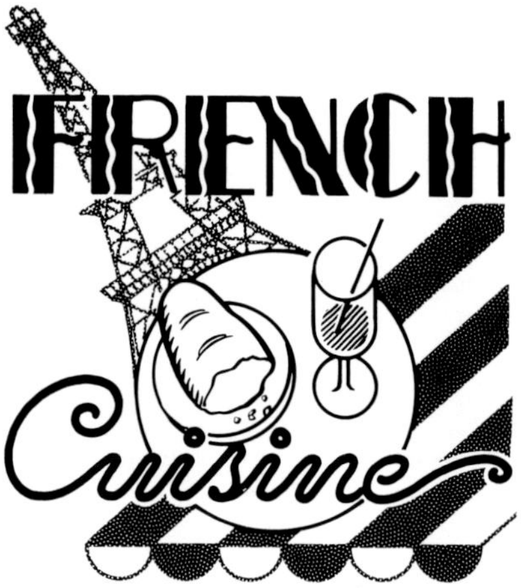

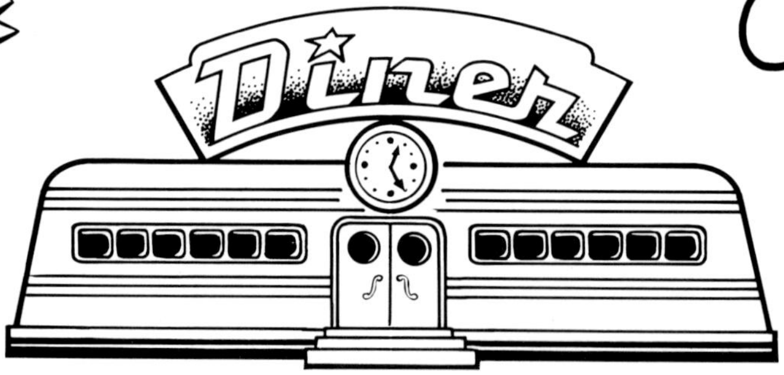

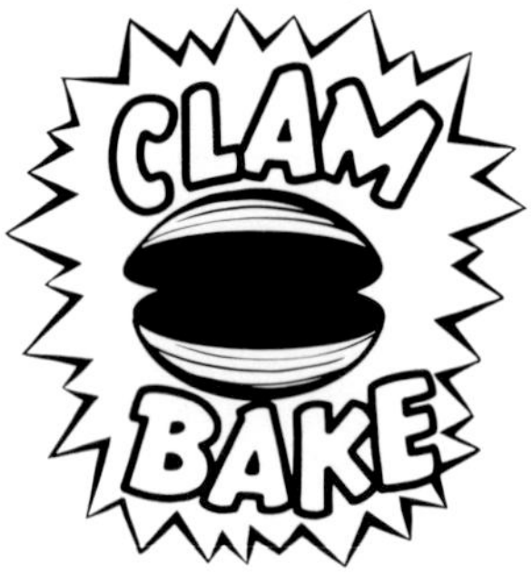

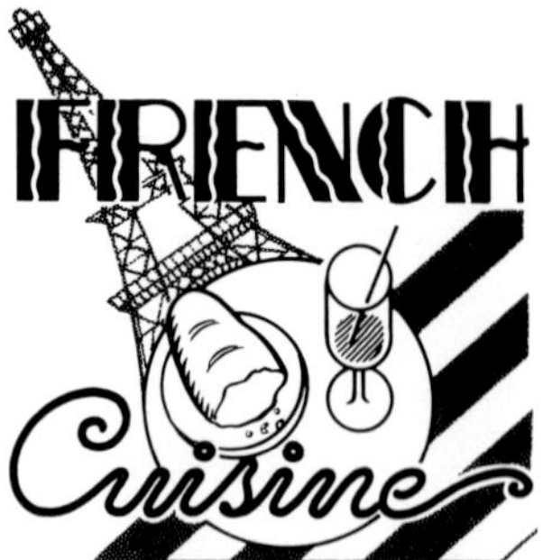

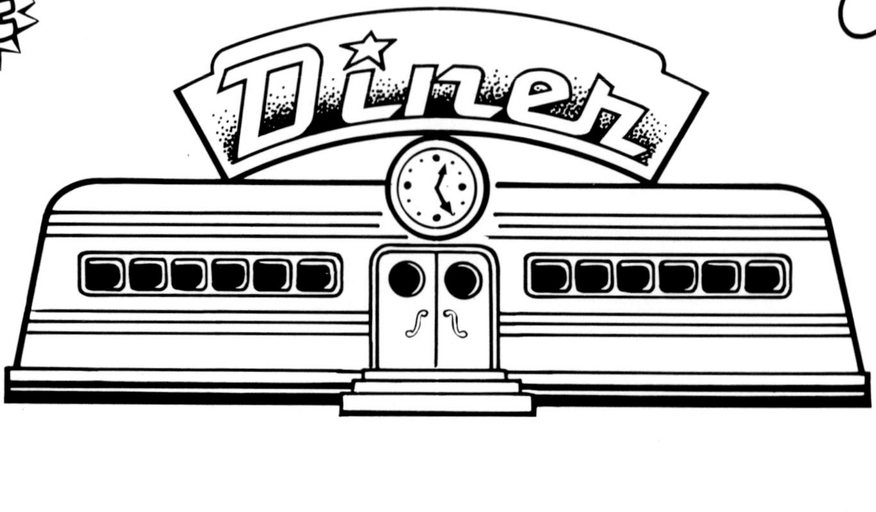

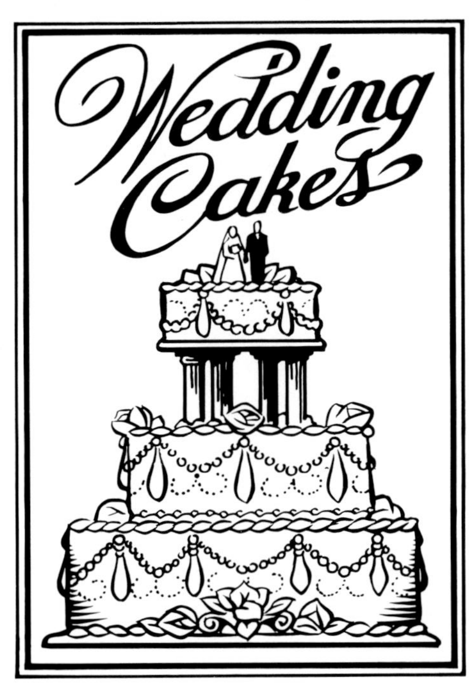
Wedding
Cakes

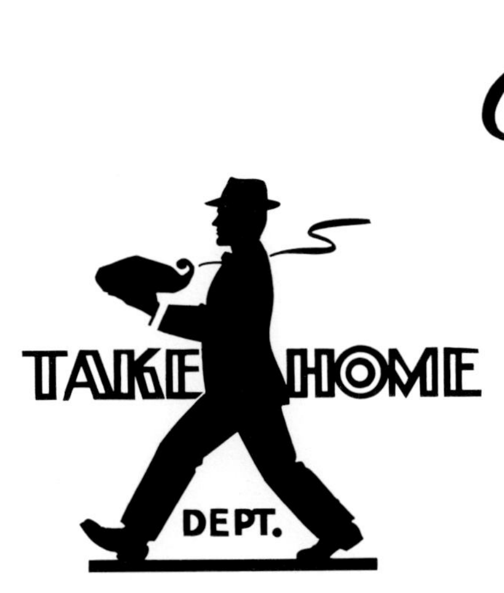
TAKE HOME
DEPT.

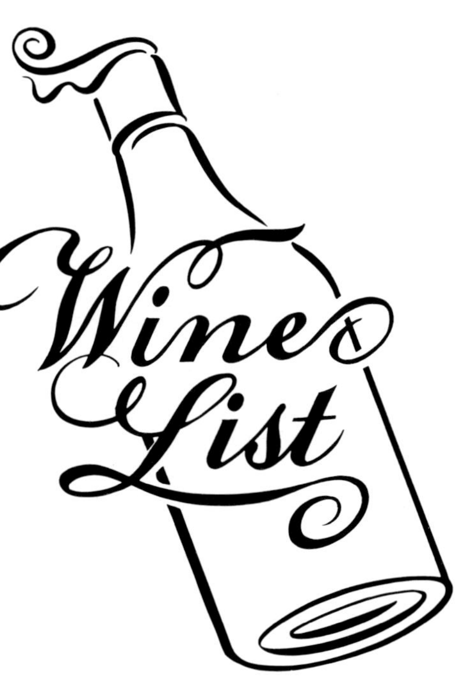
Wine
&
List

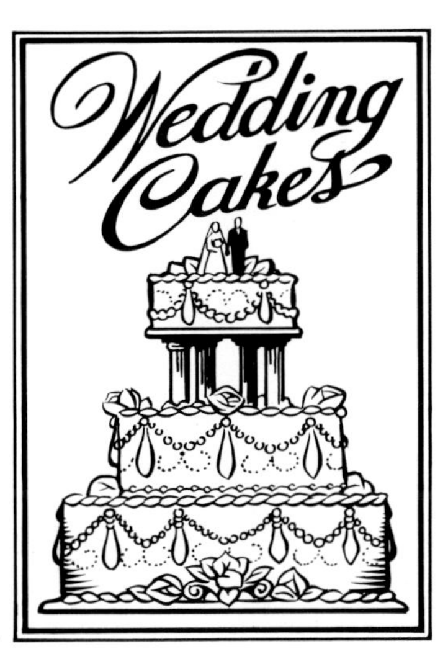
Wedding
Cakes

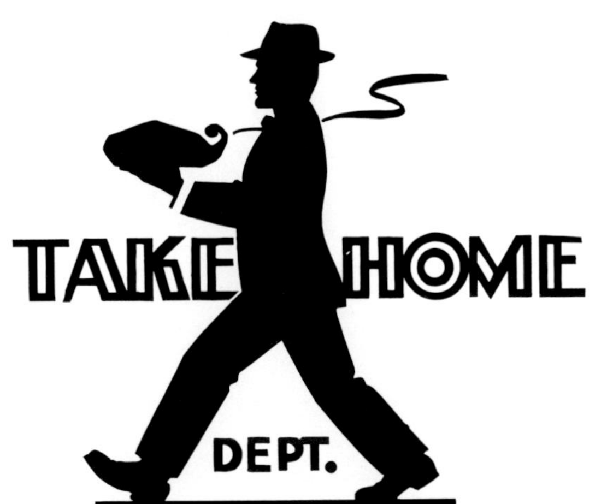
TAKE HOME
DEPT.

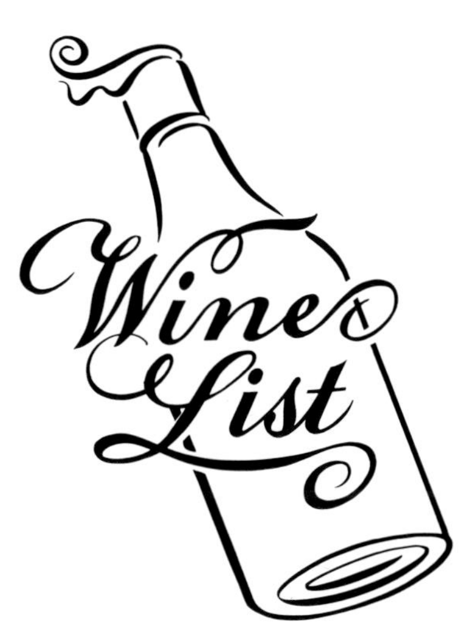
Wine
&
List

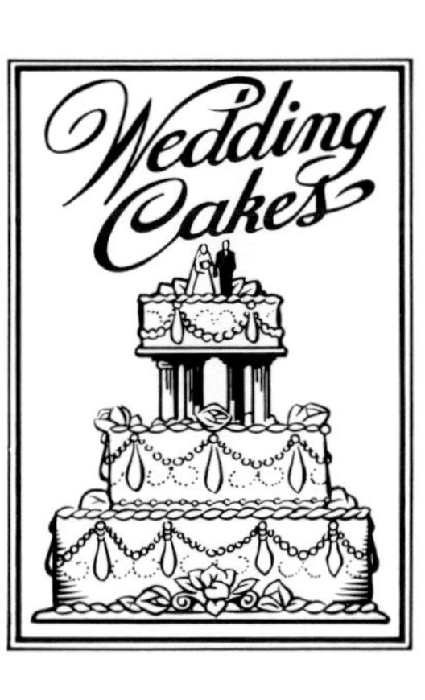
Wedding
Cakes

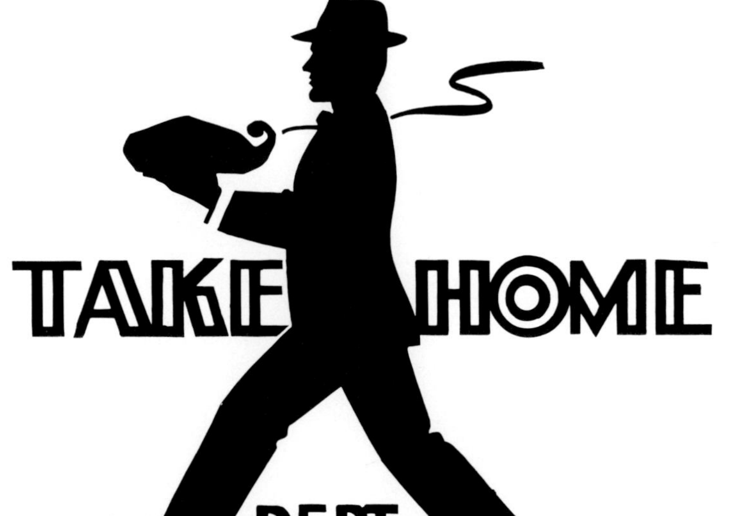
TAKE HOME
DEPT.

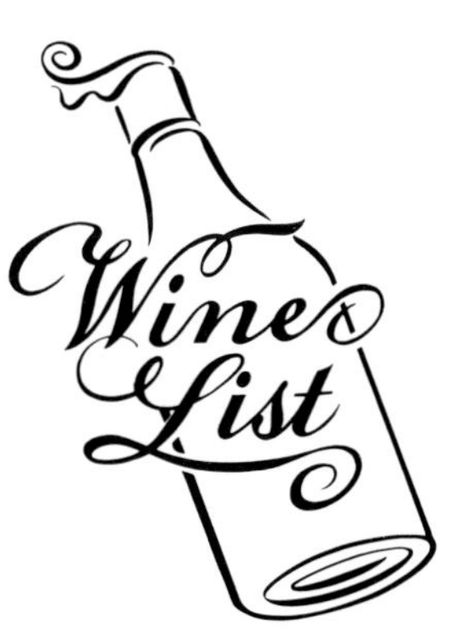
Wine
&
List

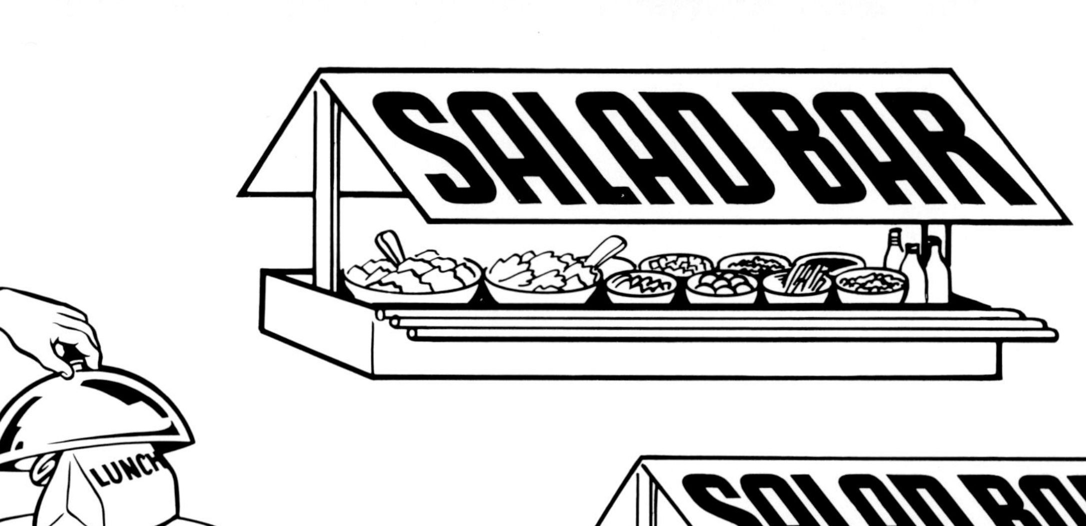
SALAD BAR

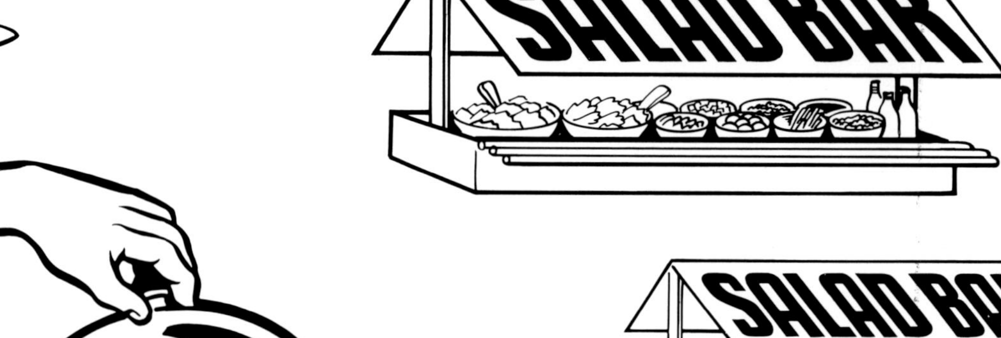
SALAD BAR

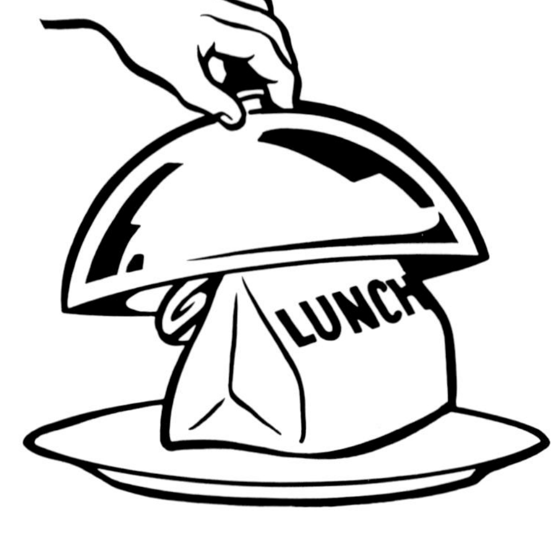
LUNCH

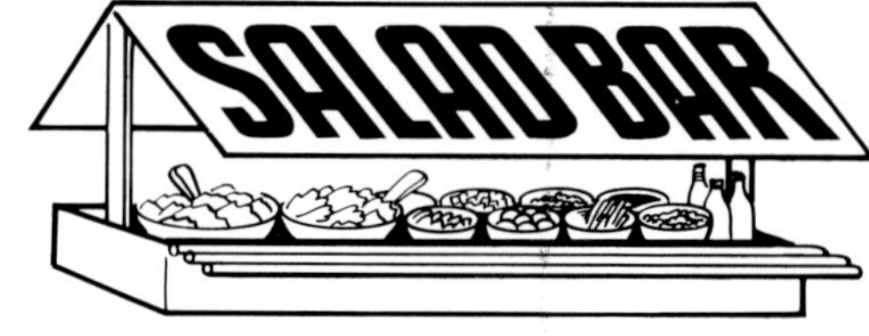
SALAD BAR

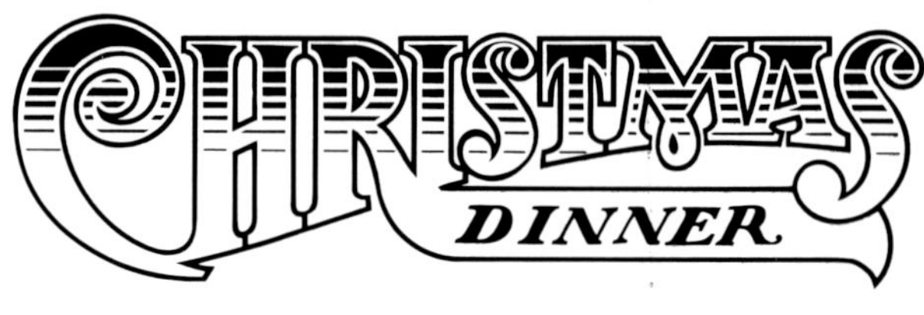
CHRISTMAS
DINNER

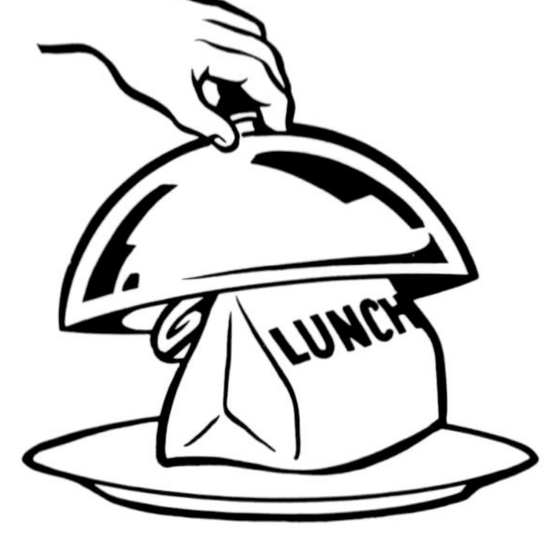
LUNCH

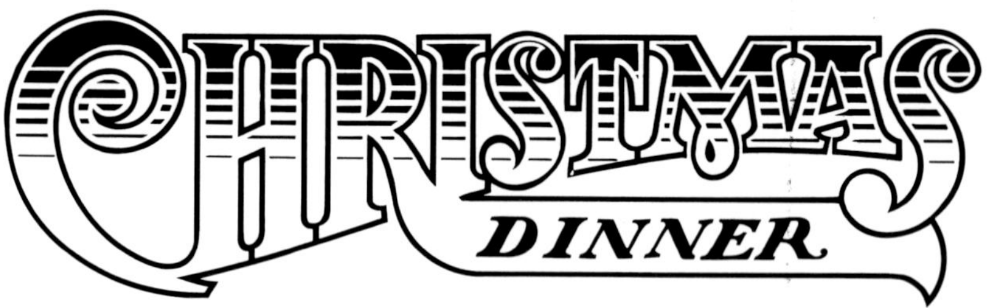
CHRISTMAS
DINNER

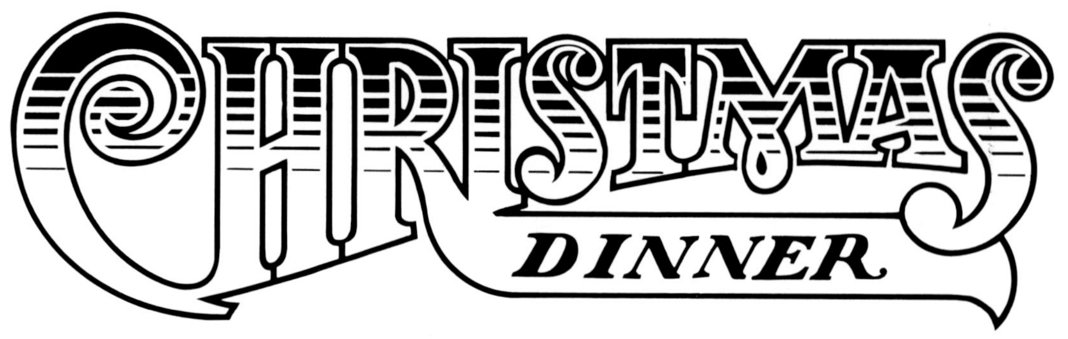
CHRISTMAS
DINNER

SANDWICHES

SANDWICHES

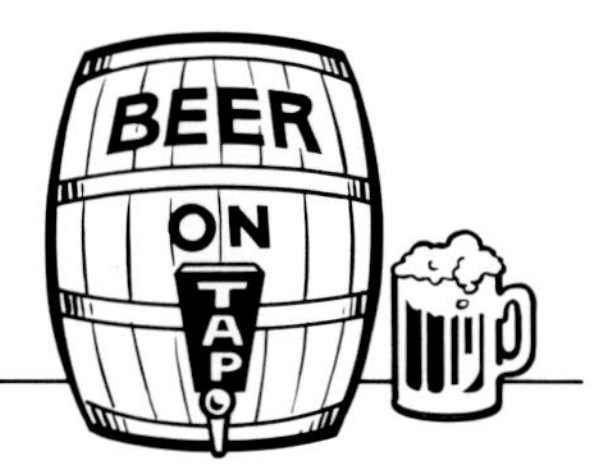

SANDWICHES

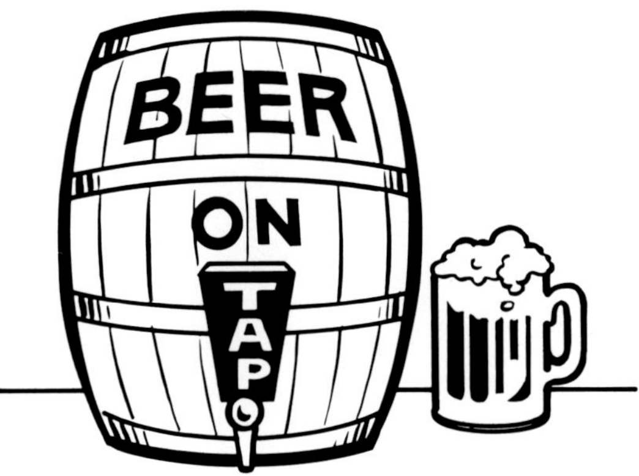

FRESH SEAFOOD

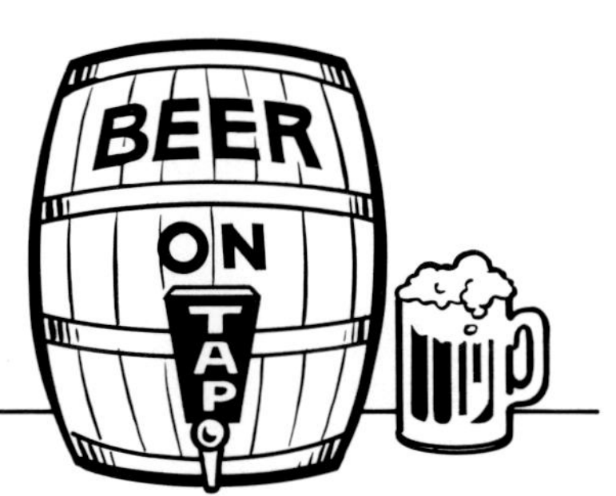

FRESH SEAFOOD

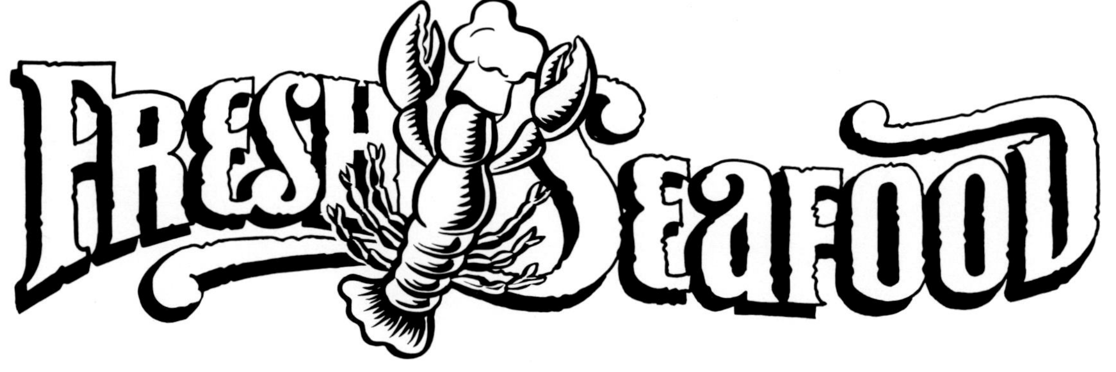

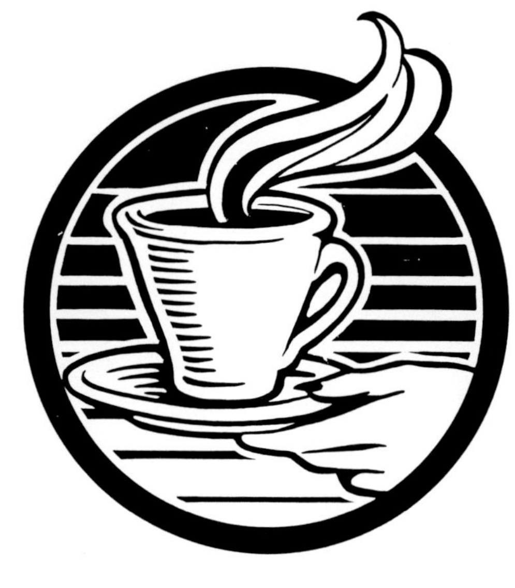
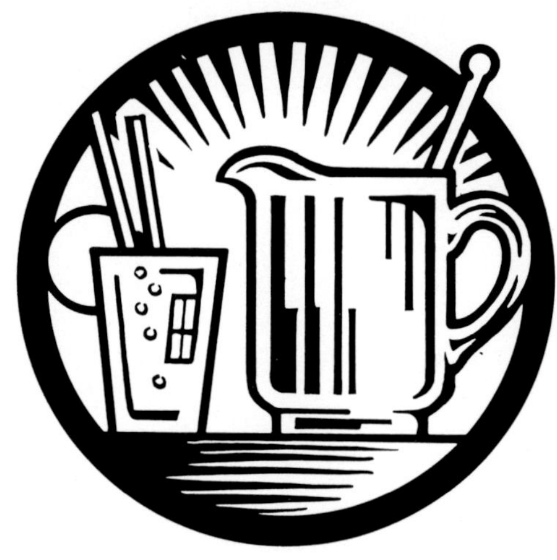
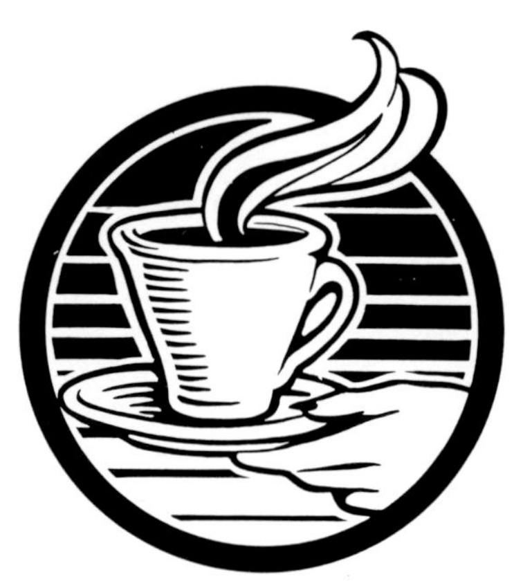
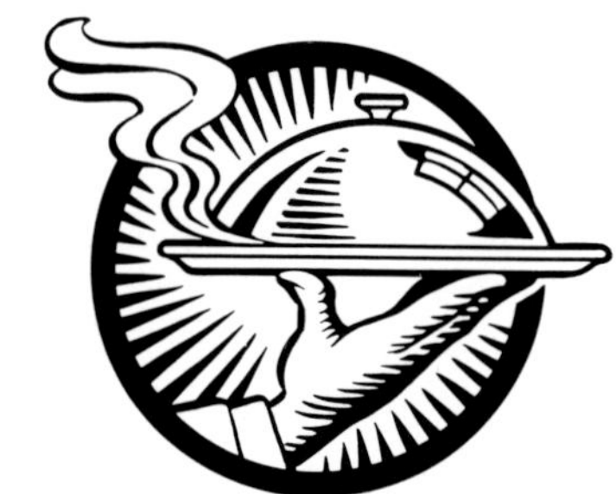
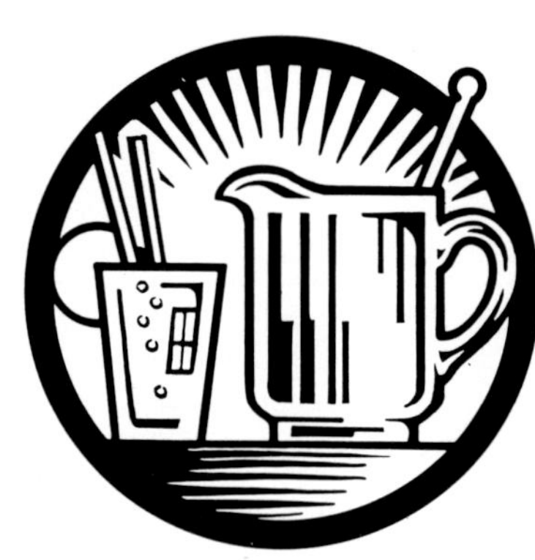
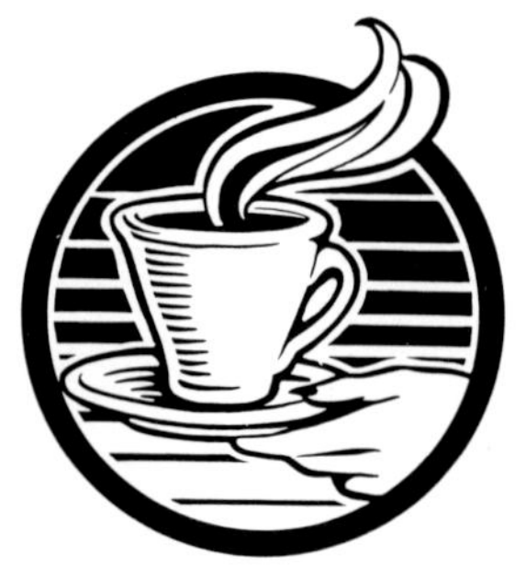
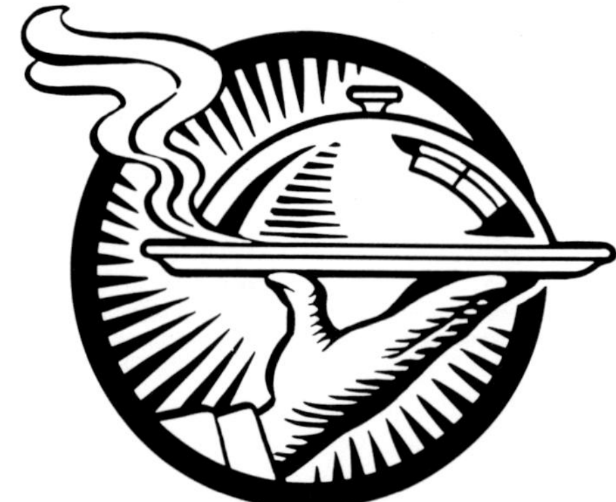
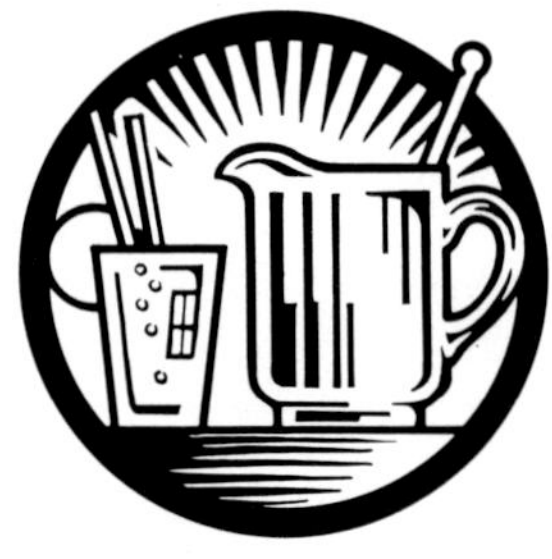
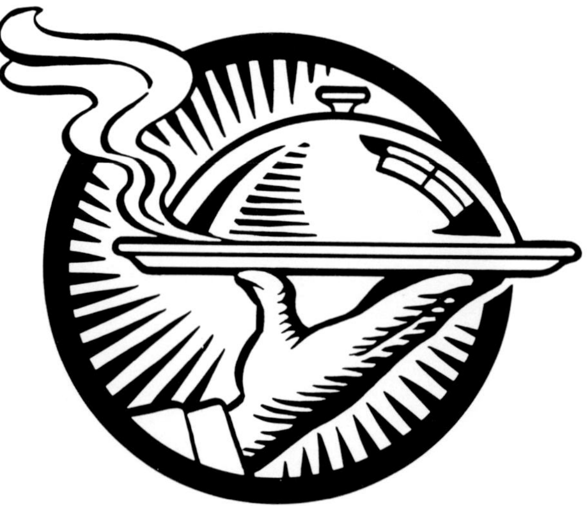

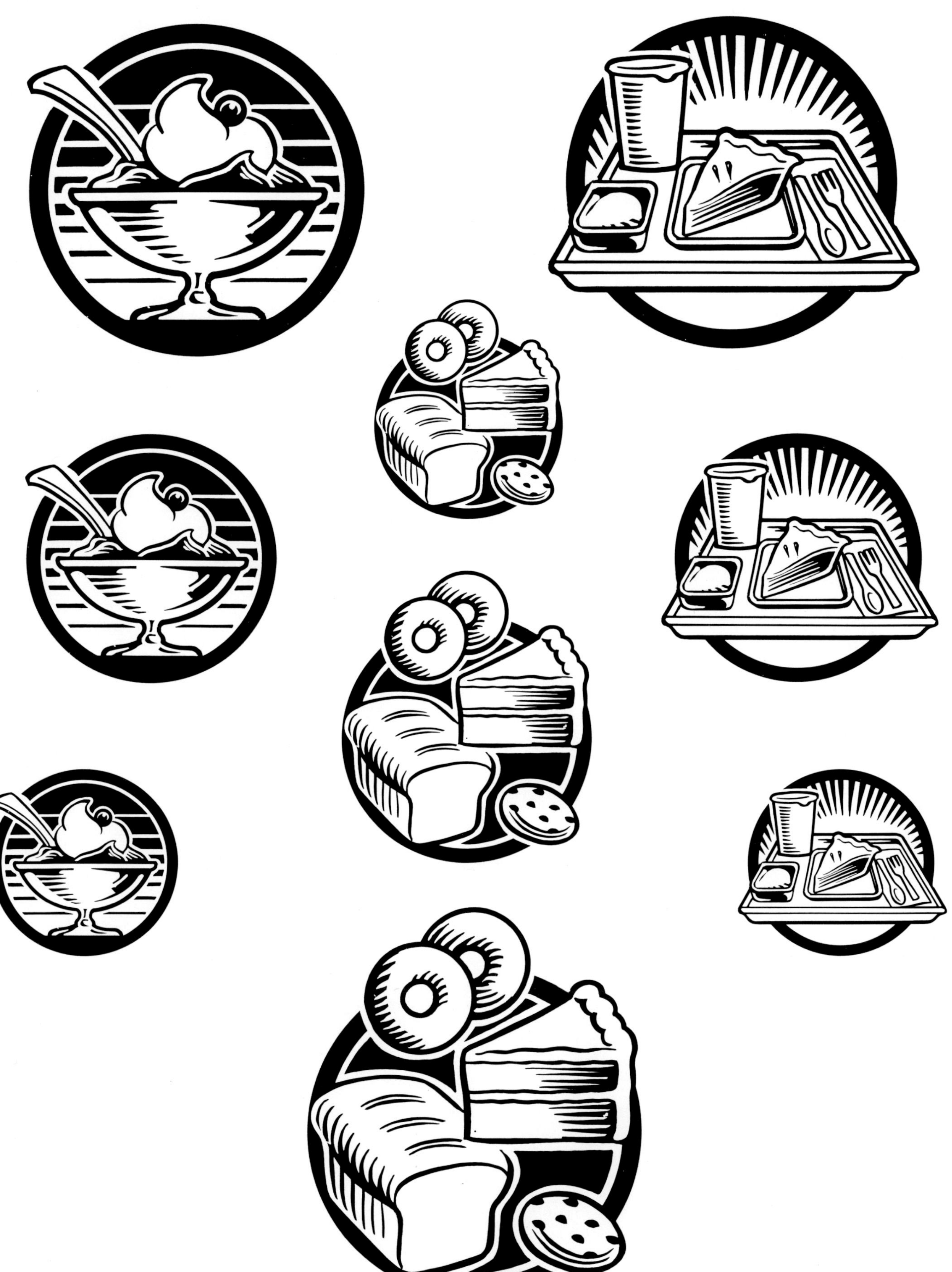

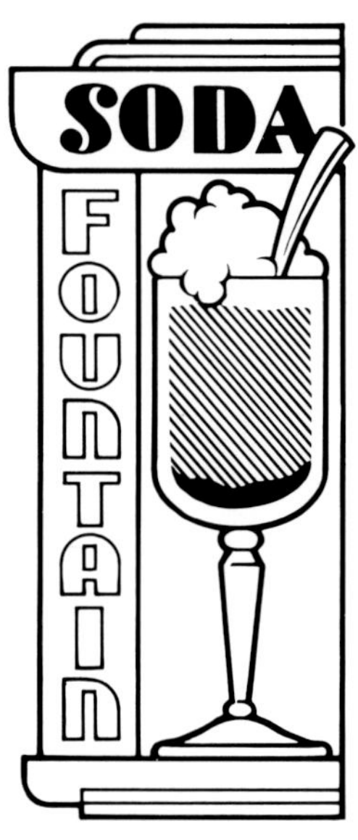
SODA
FOUNTAIN

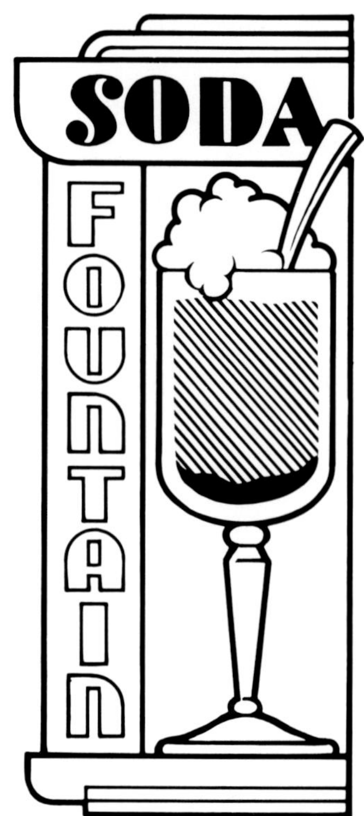
SODA
FOUNTAIN

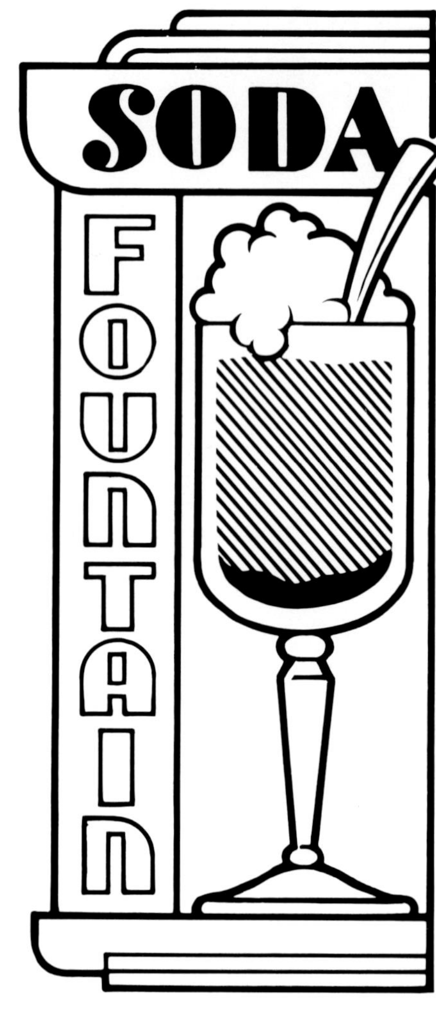
SODA
FOUNTAIN

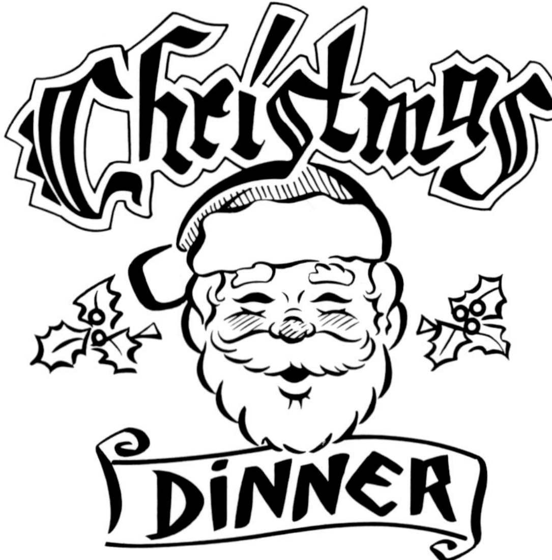
Christmas
DINNER

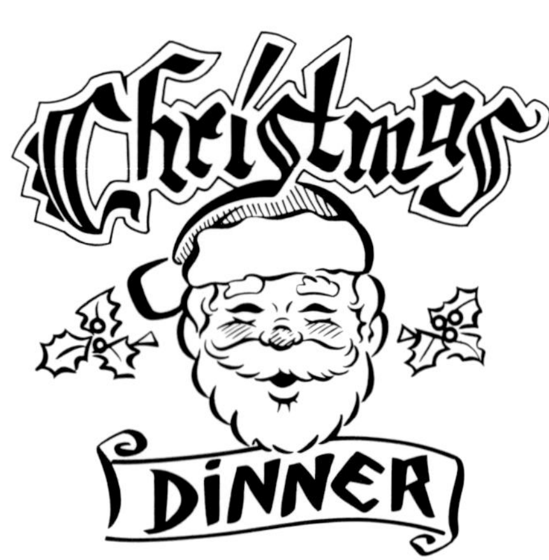
Christmas
DINNER

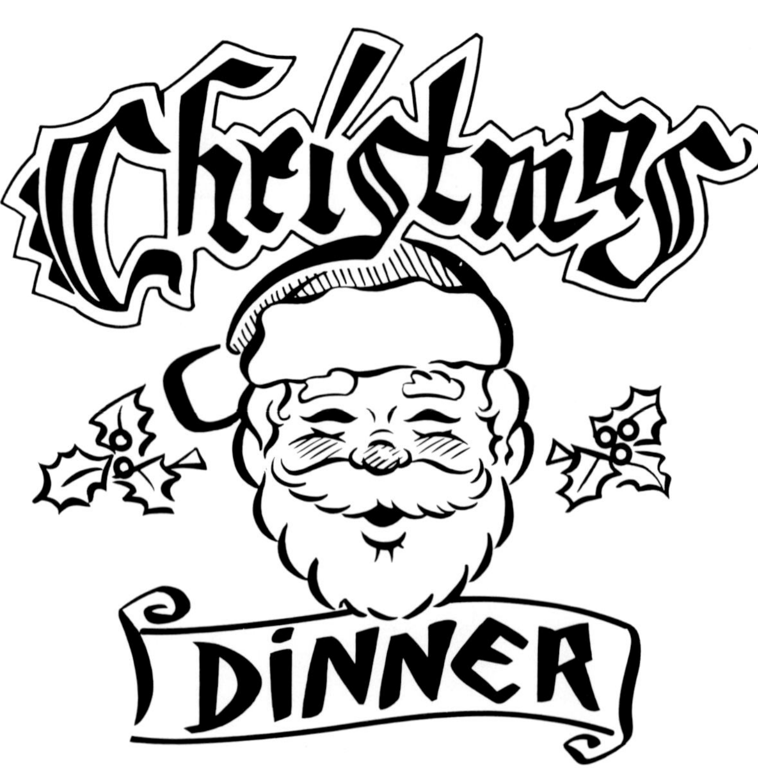
Christmas
DINNER

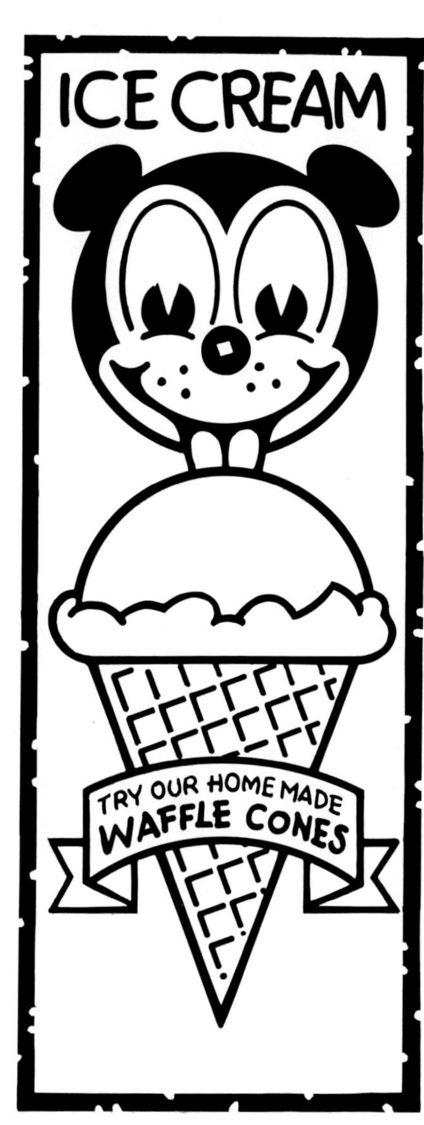
ICE CREAM
TRY OUR HOME MADE
WAFFLE CONES

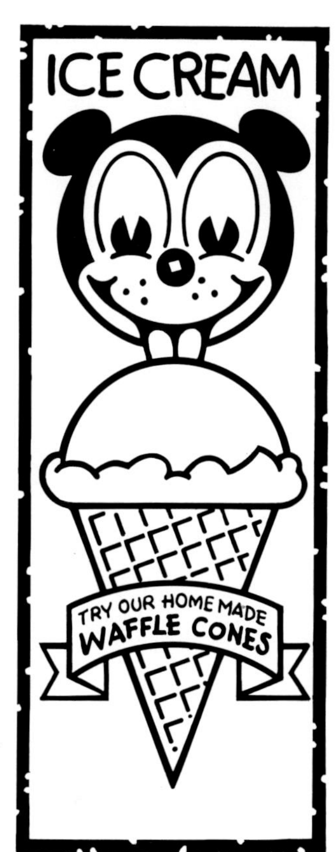
ICE CREAM
TRY OUR HOME MADE
WAFFLE CONES

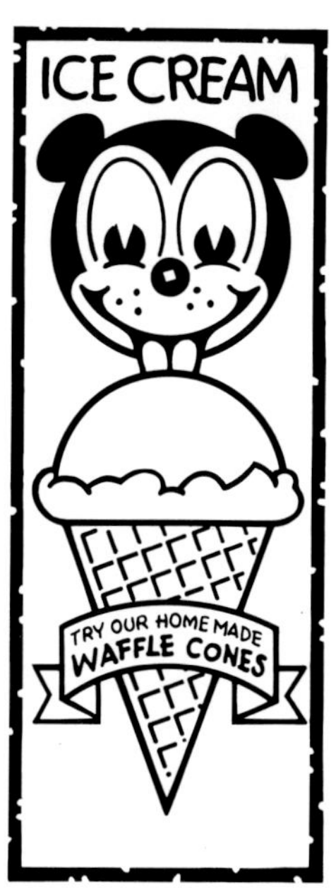
ICE CREAM
TRY OUR HOME MADE
WAFFLE CONES

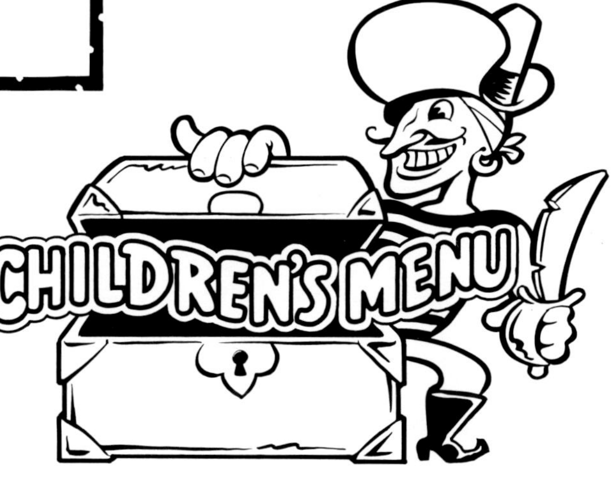
CHILDREN'S MENU

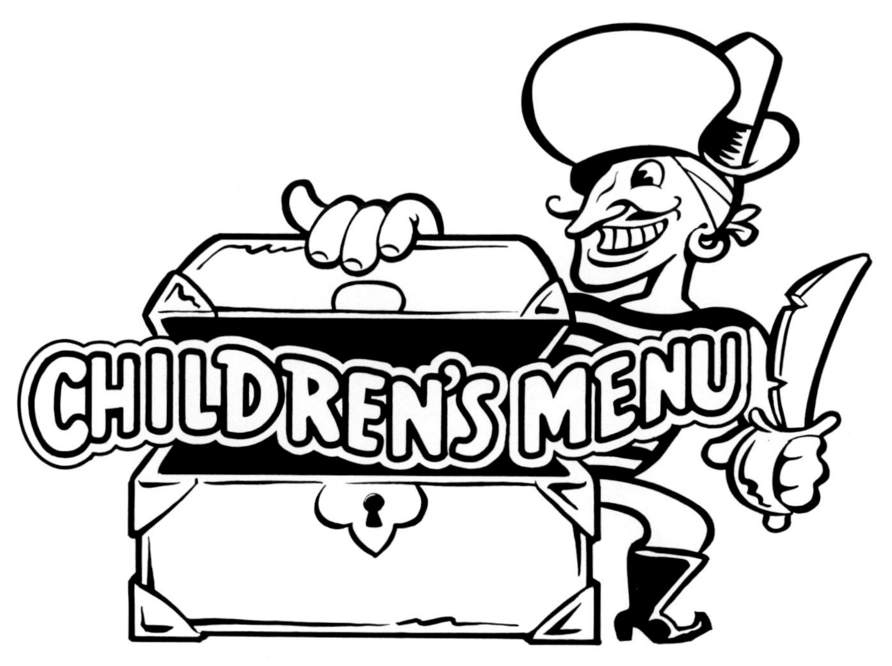
CHILDREN'S MENU

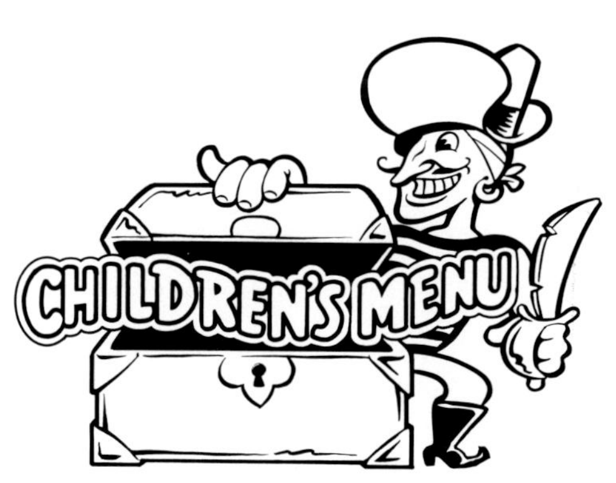
CHILDREN'S MENU

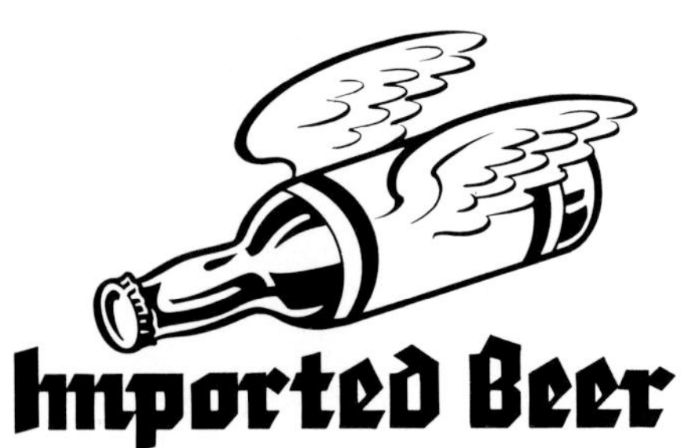
Imported Beer

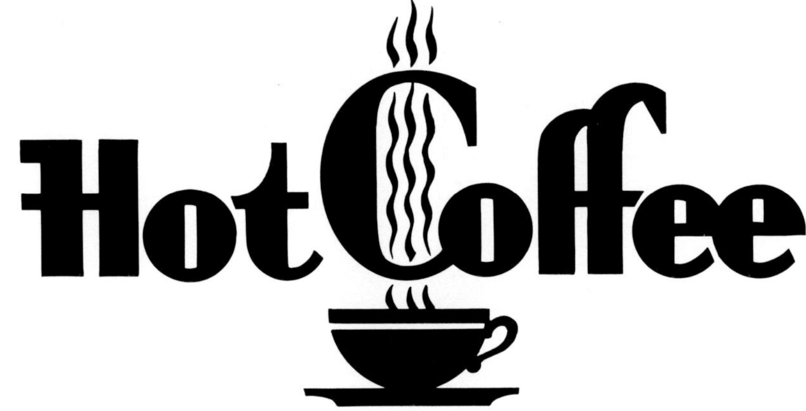
Hot Coffee

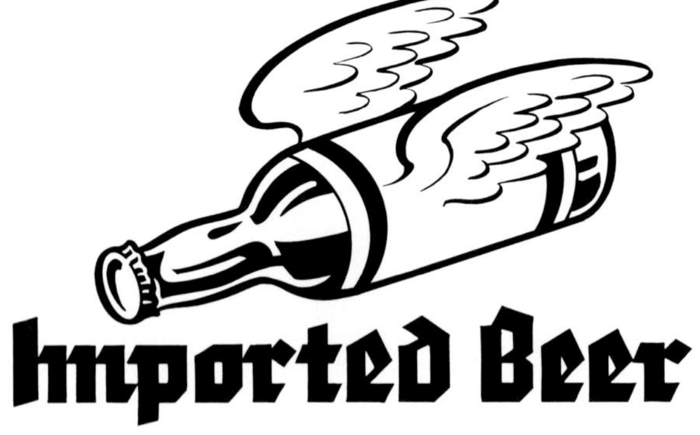
Imported Beer

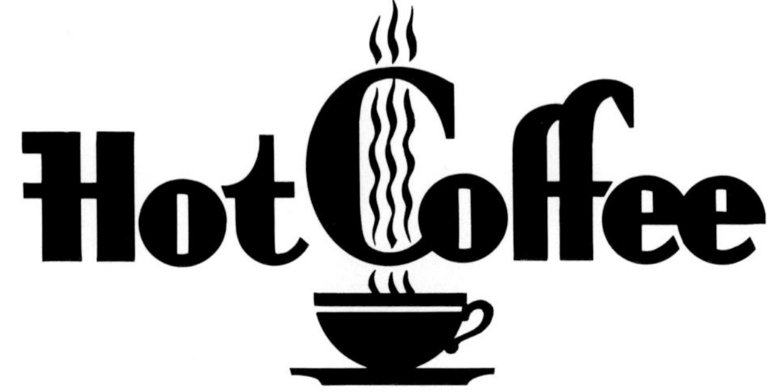
Hot Coffee

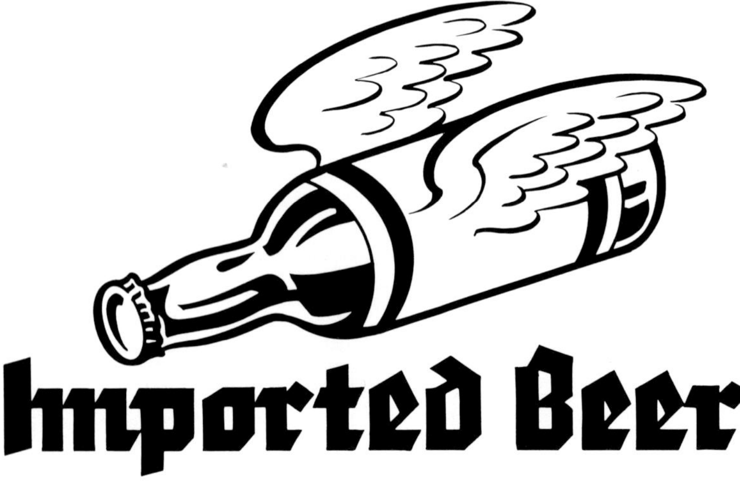
Imported Beer

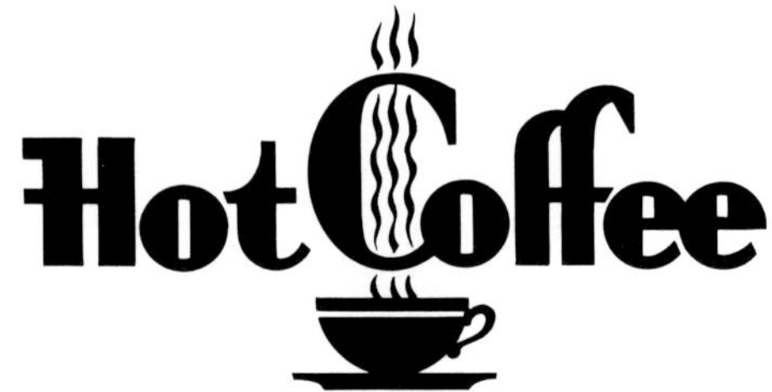
Hot Coffee

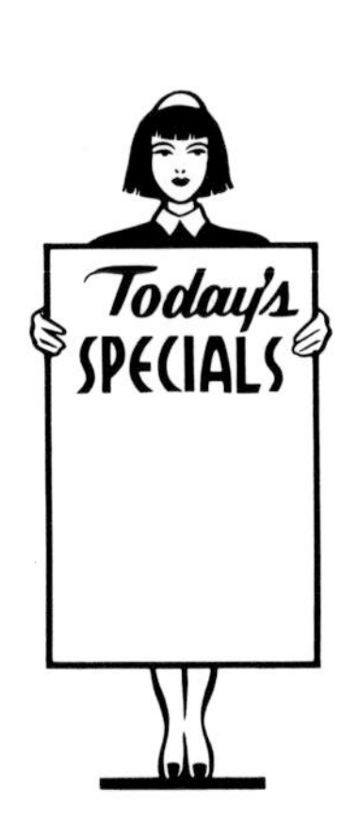
Today's
SPECIALS

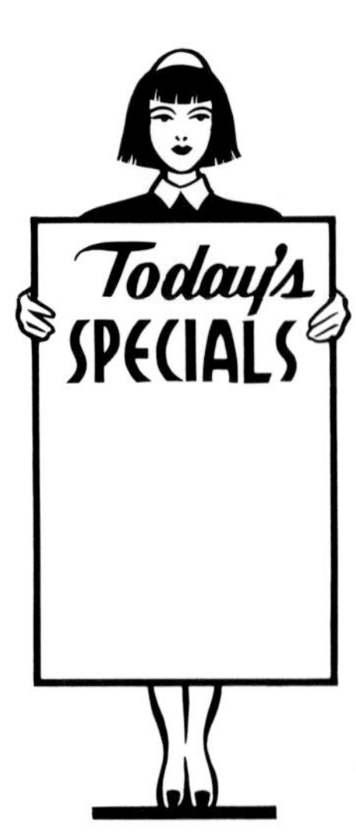
Today's
SPECIALS

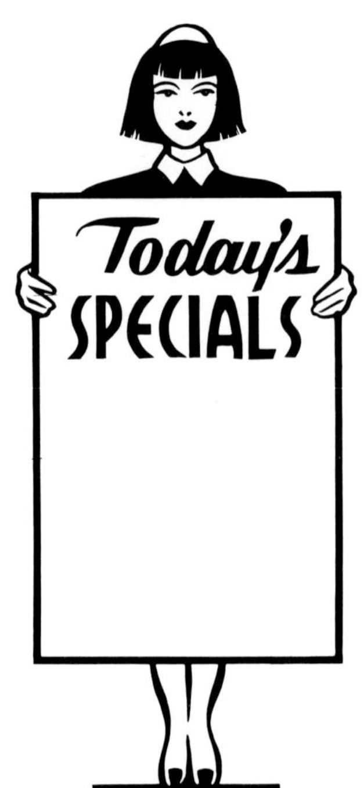
Today's
SPECIALS

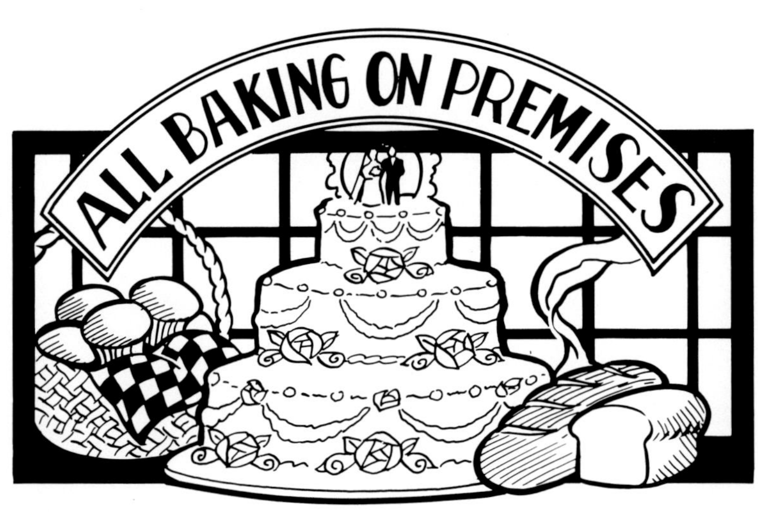
ALL BAKING ON PREMISES

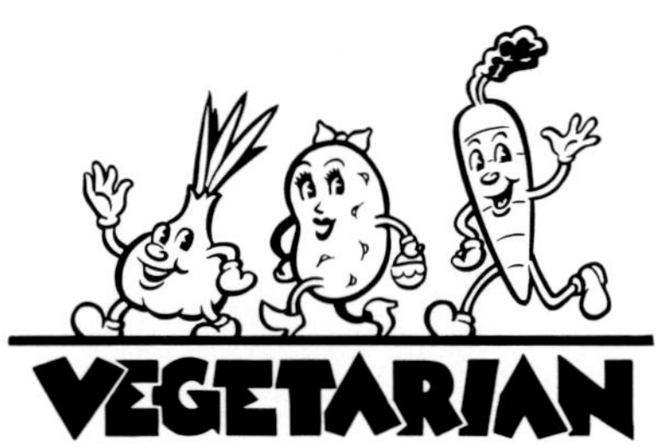
VEGETARIAN

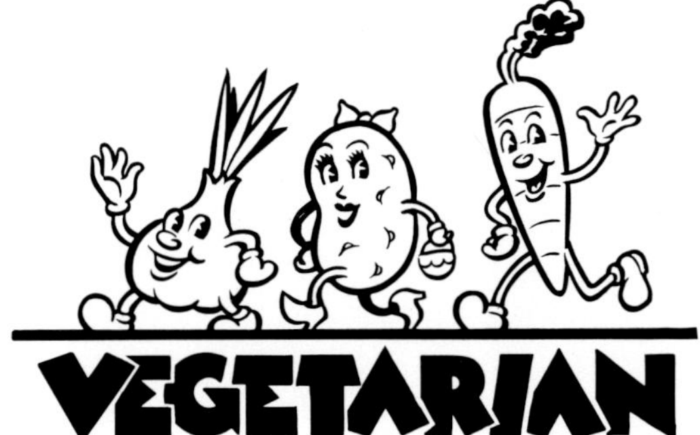
VEGETARIAN

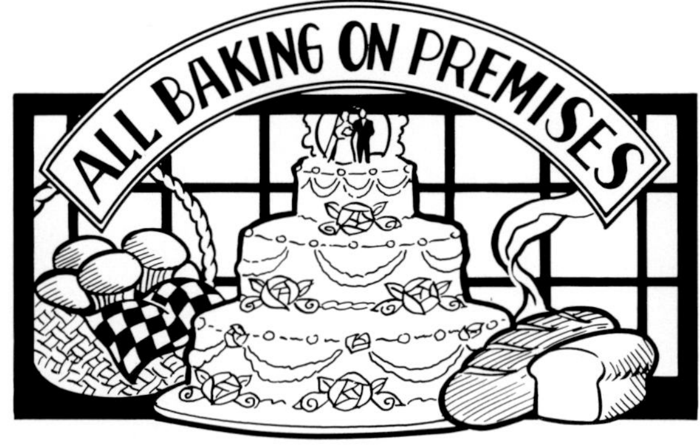
ALL BAKING ON PREMISES

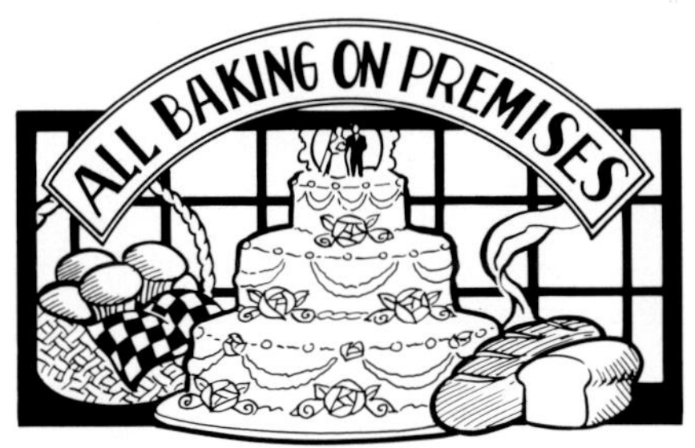
ALL BAKING ON PREMISES

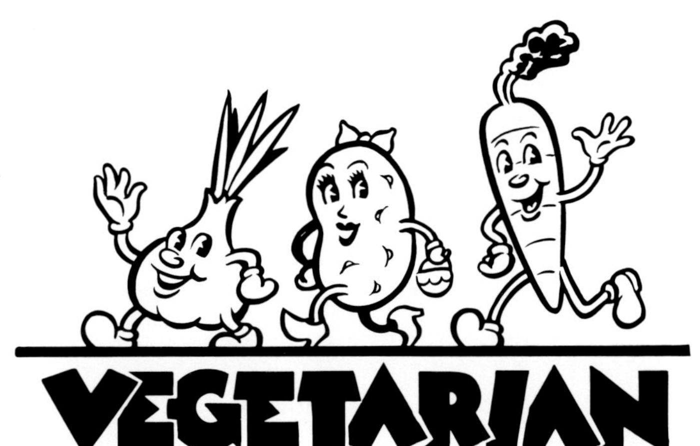
VEGETARIAN

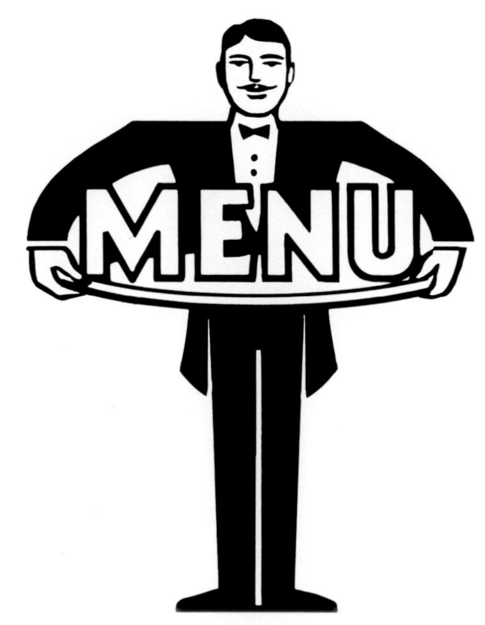
MENU

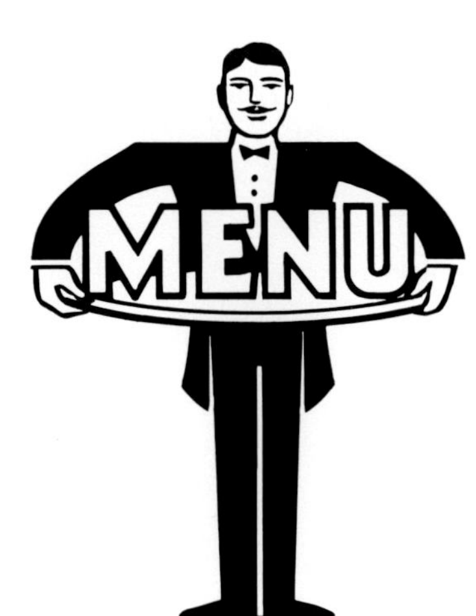
MENU

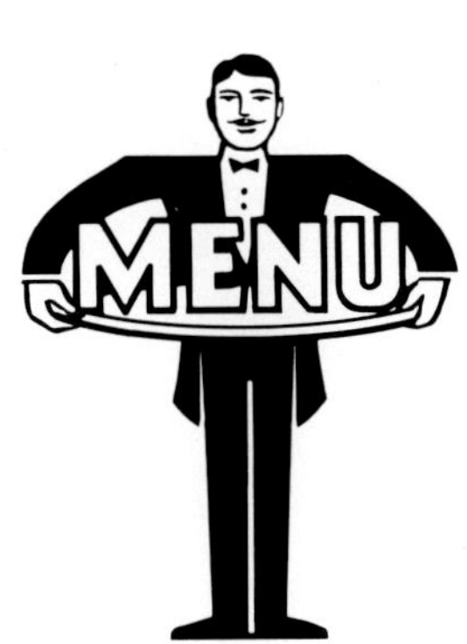
MENU

Bistro

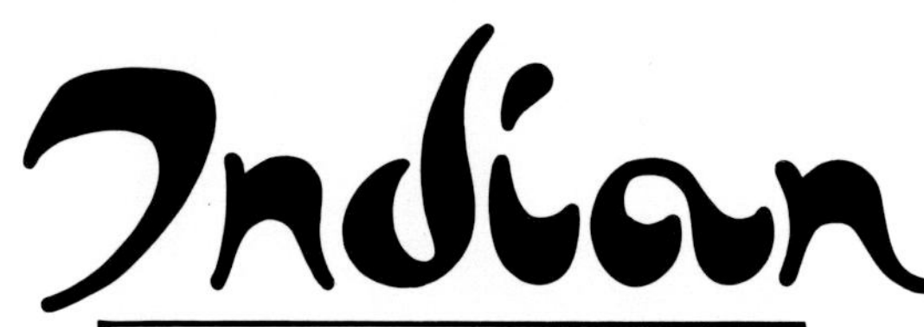

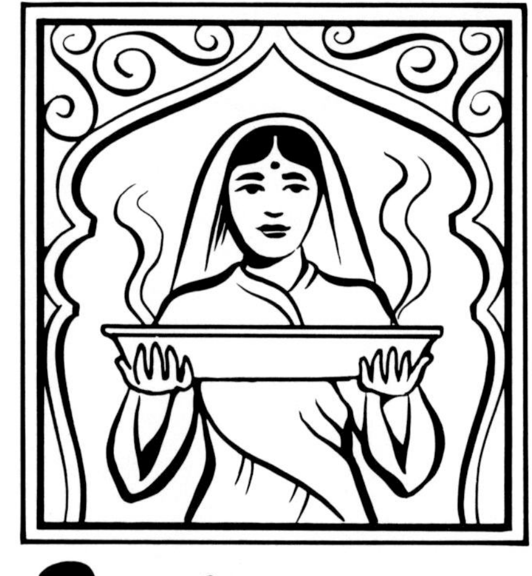

Restaurant

Bistro

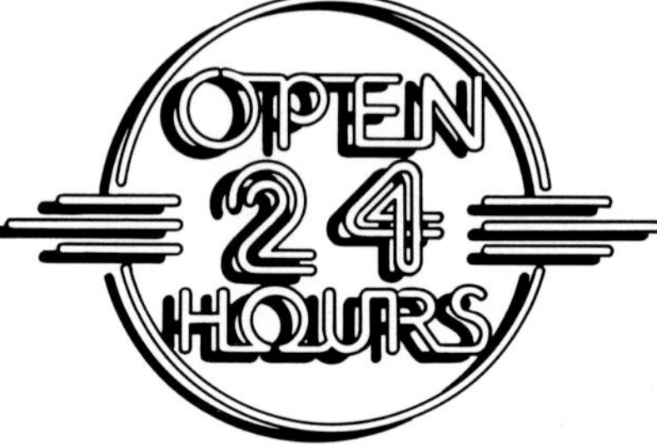

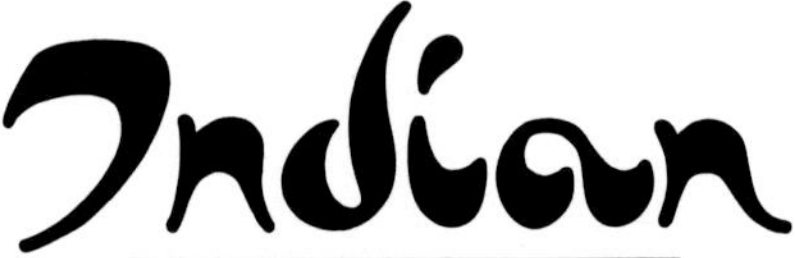

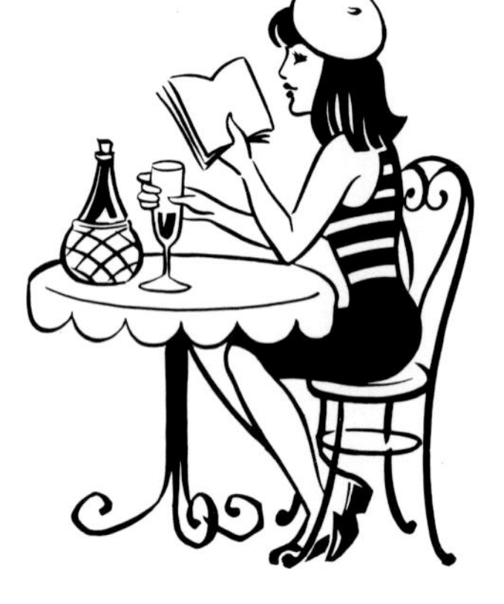

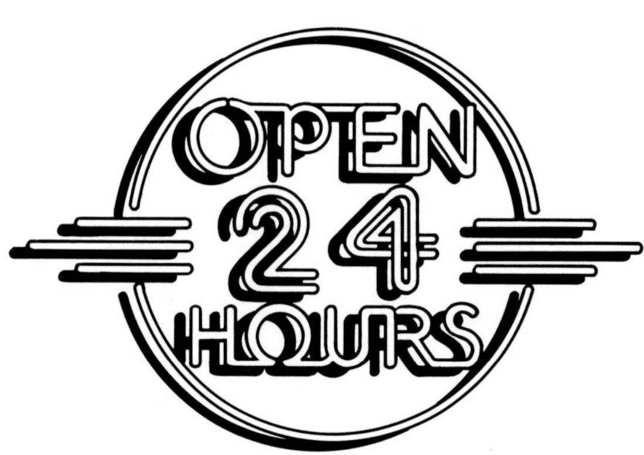

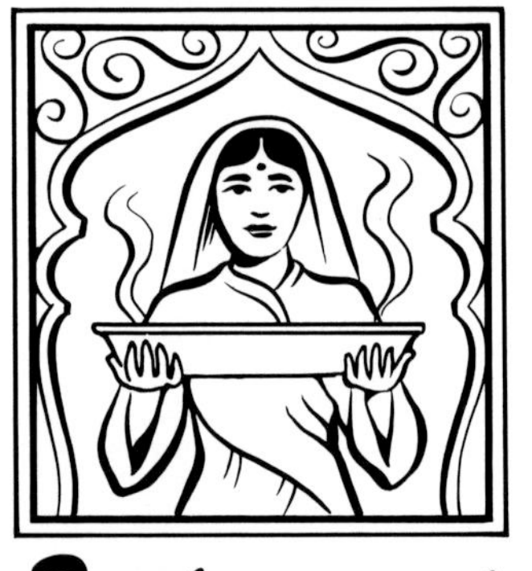

Restaurant

Bistro

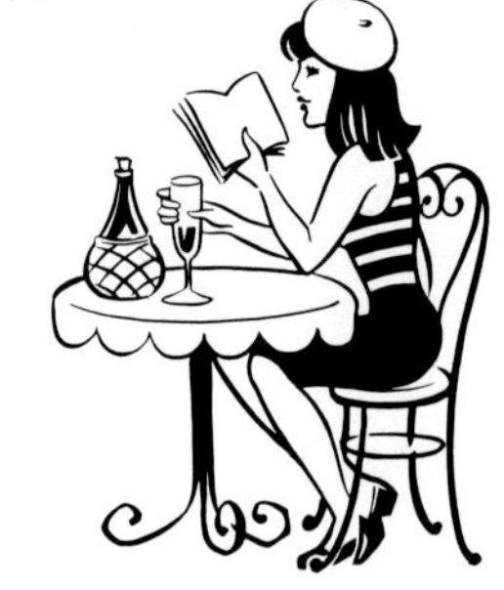

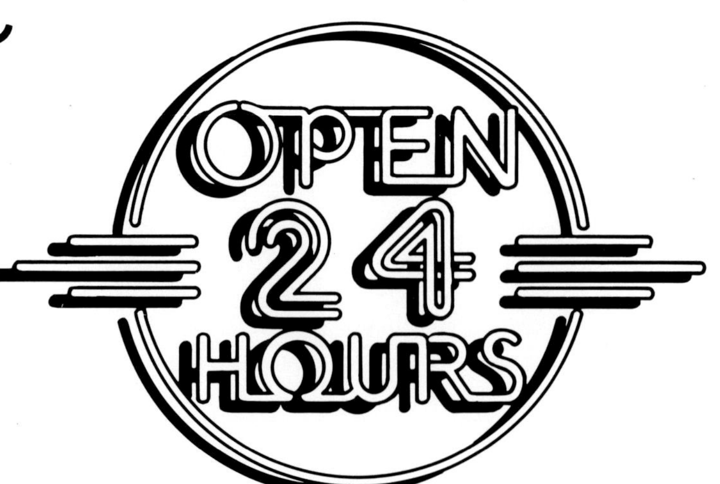

Indian

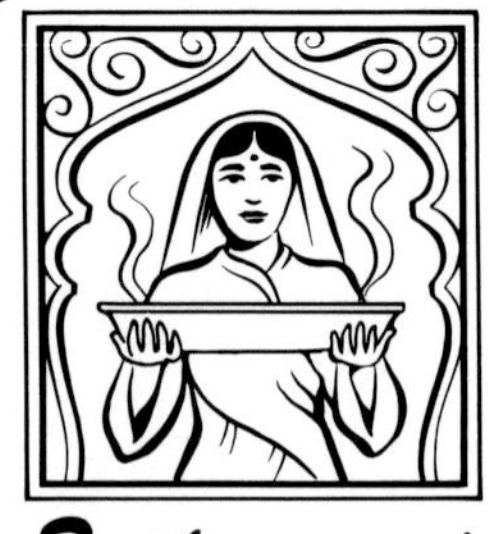

Restaurant

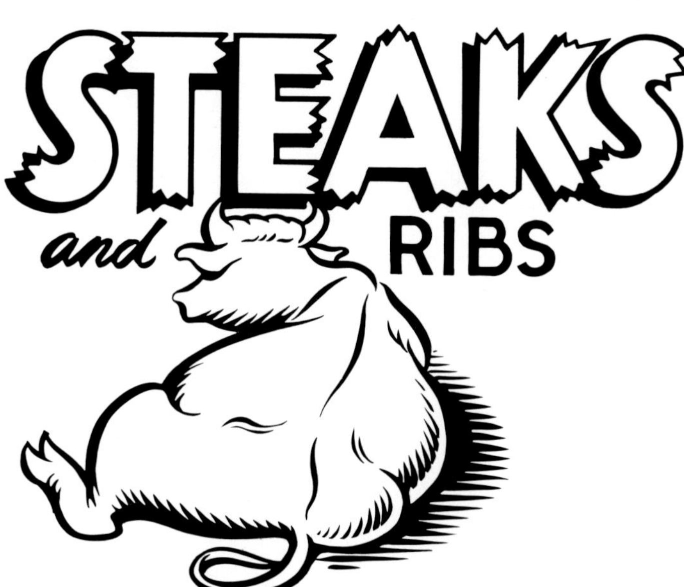
STEAKS
and
RIBS

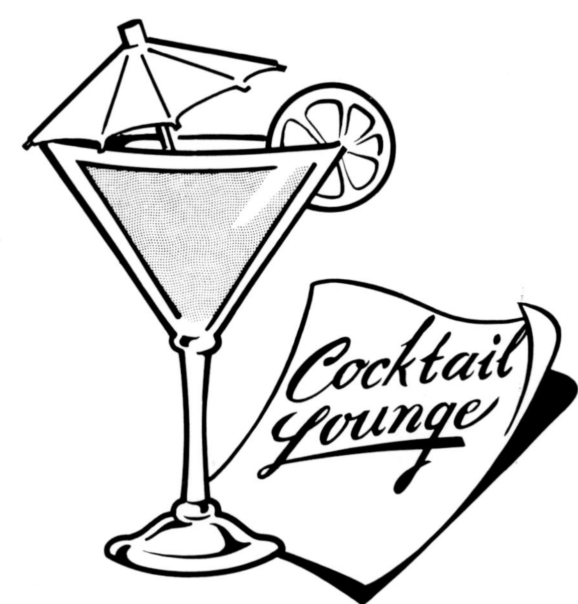
Cocktail
Lounge

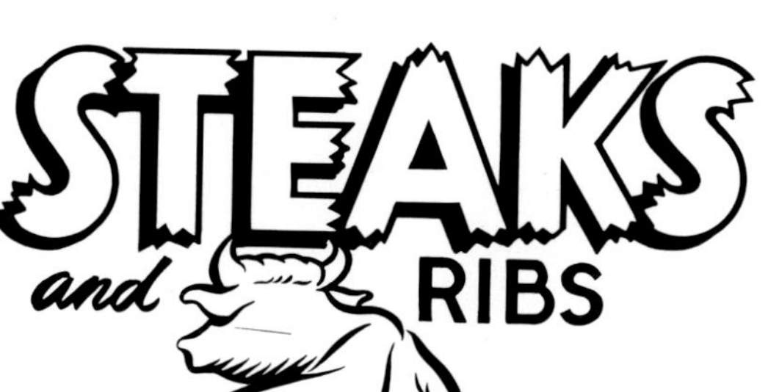
STEAKS
and
RIBS

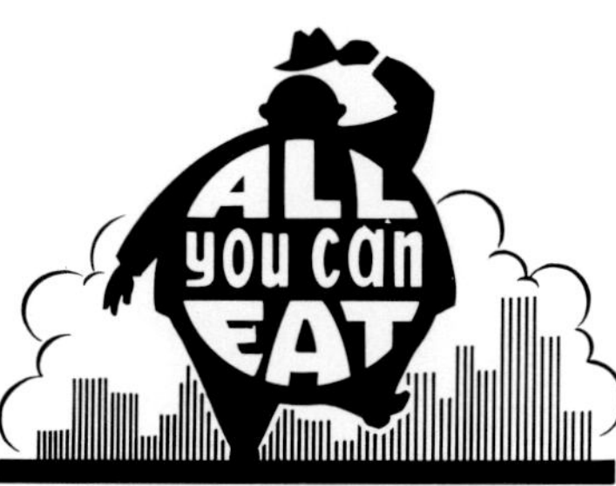
ALL
you can
EAT

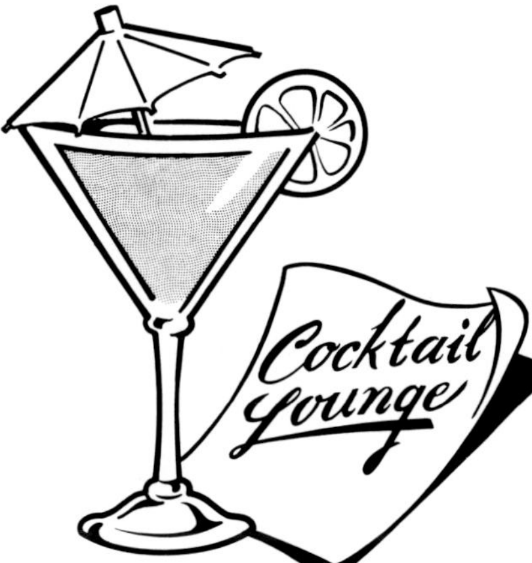
Cocktail
Lounge

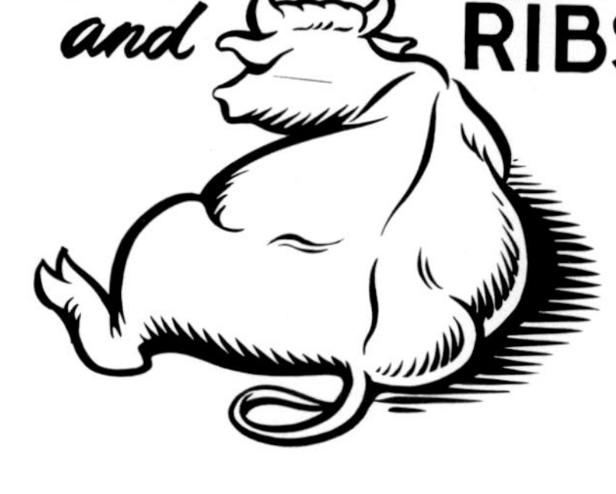
STEAKS
and
RIBS

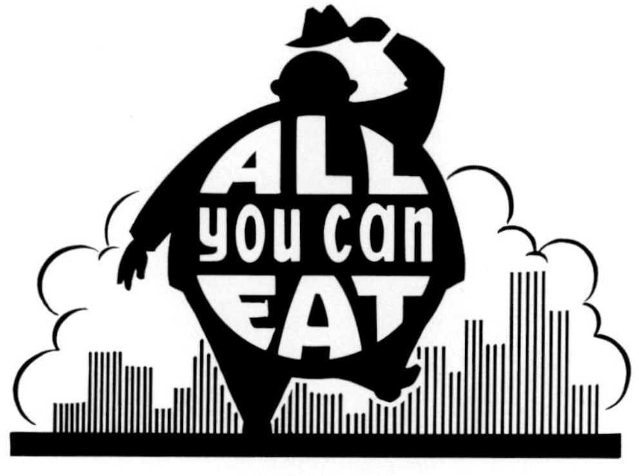
ALL
you can
EAT

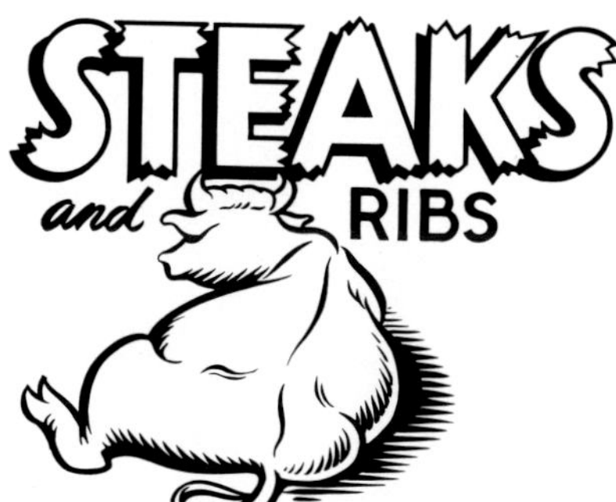

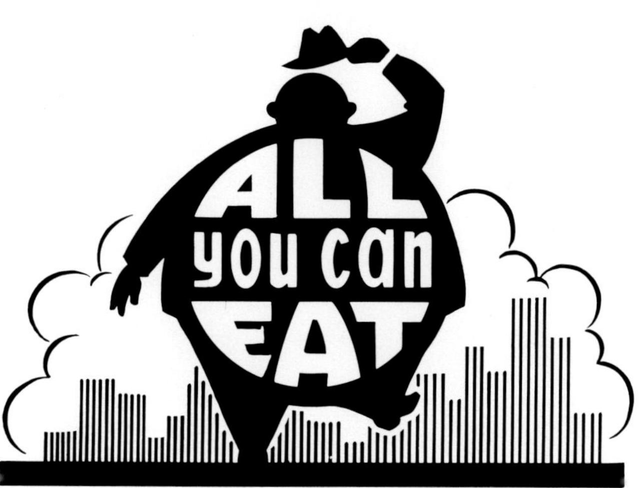
ALL
you can
EAT

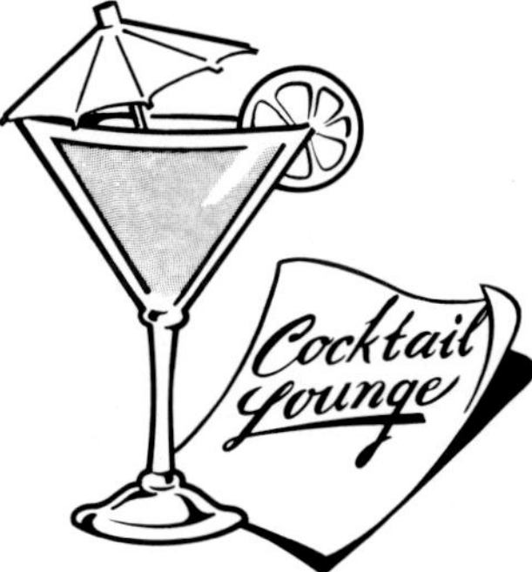
Cocktail
Lounge

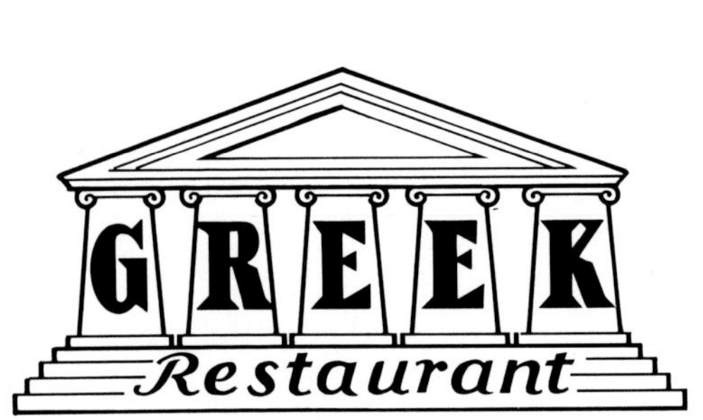
GREEK
Restaurant

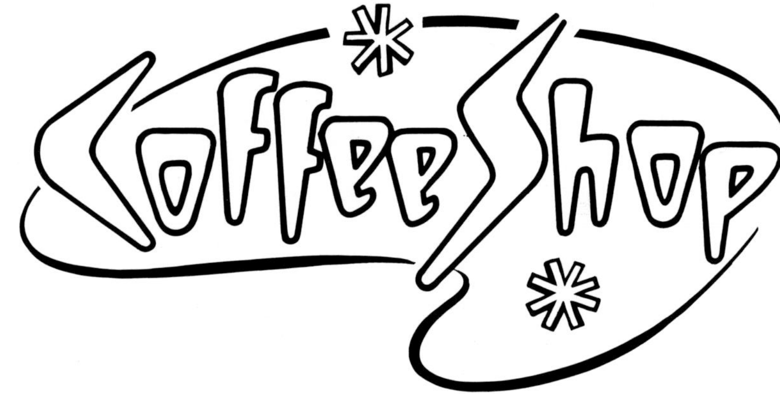
Coffee Shop

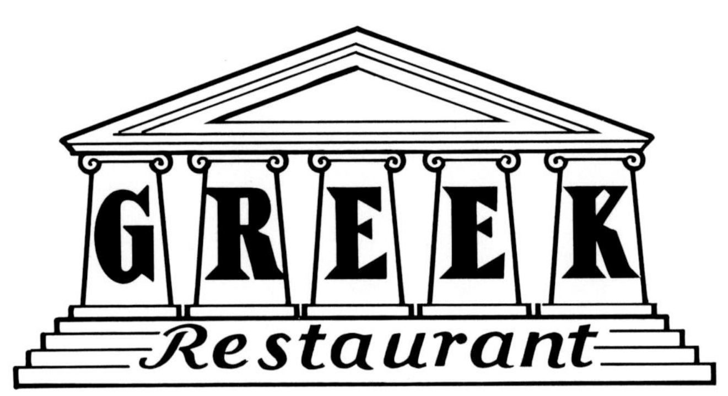
GREEK
Restaurant

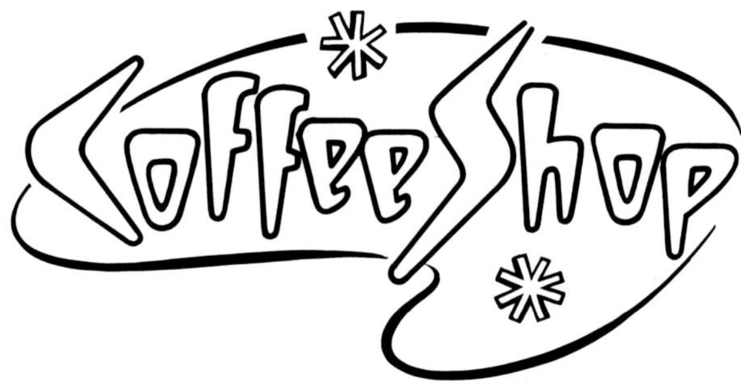
Coffee Shop

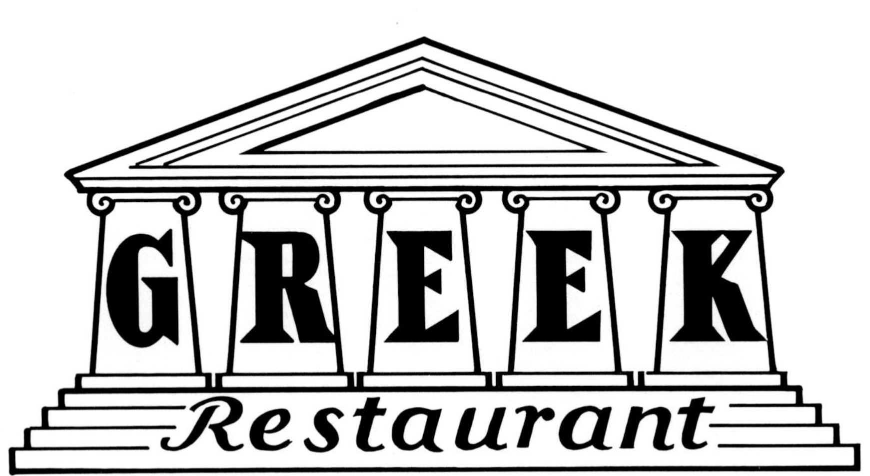
GREEK
Restaurant

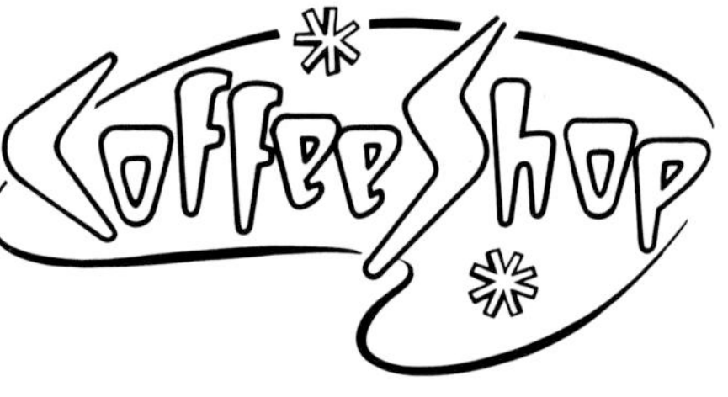
Coffee Shop

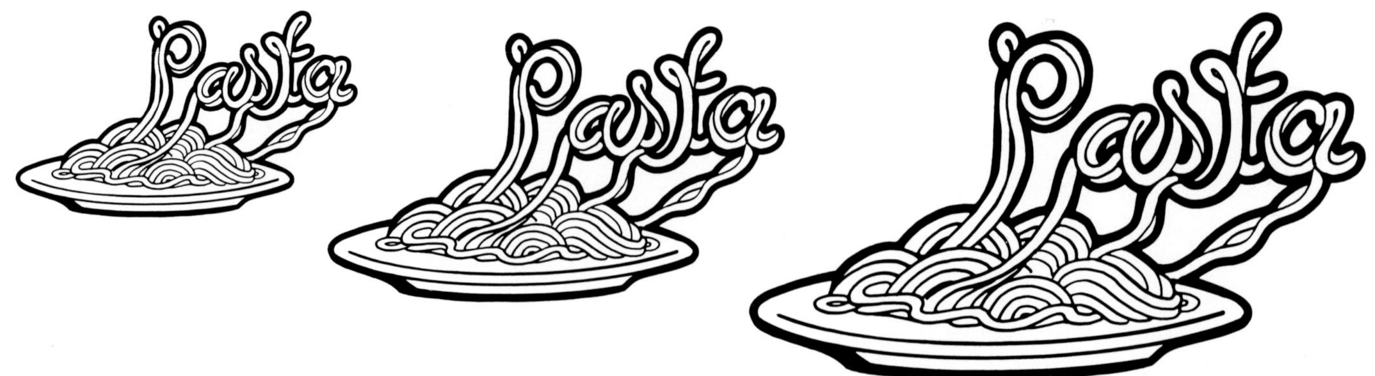
Pasta
Pasta
Pasta

Delicatessen

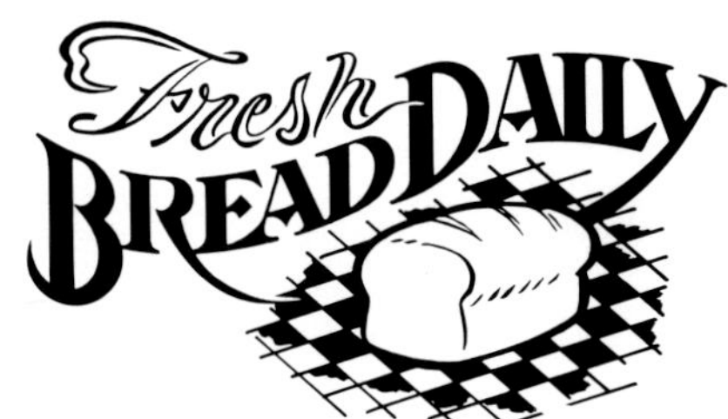

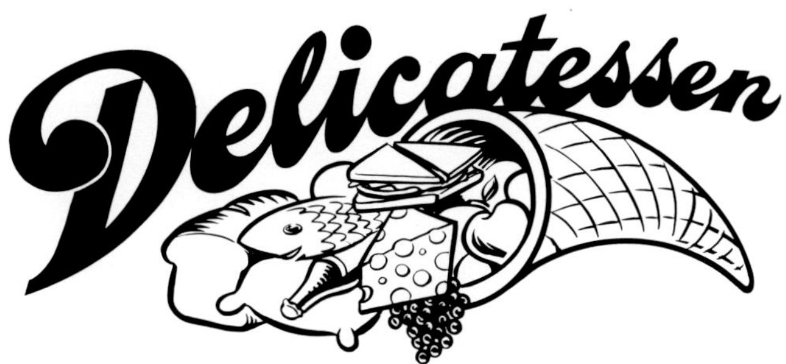

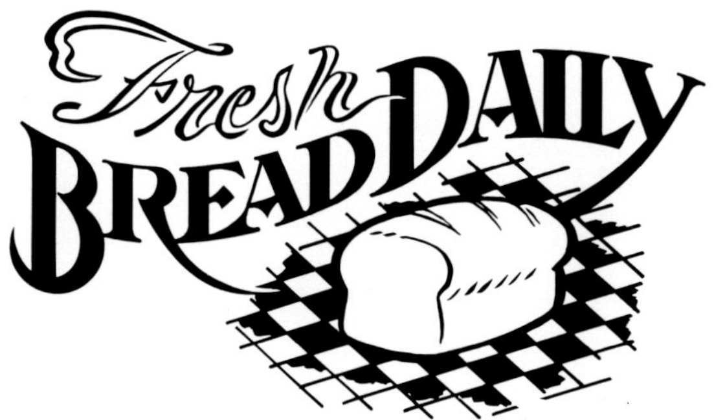

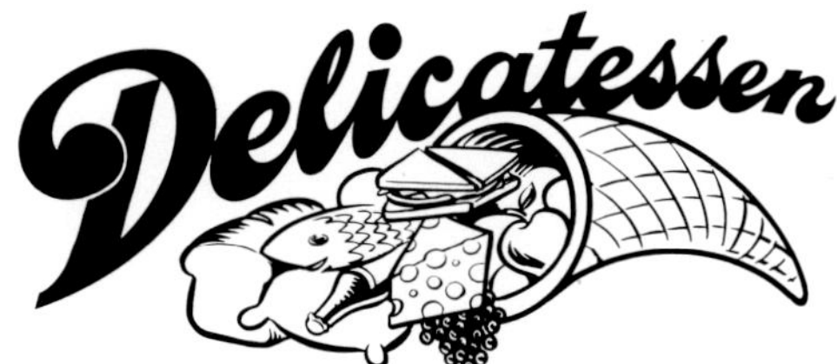

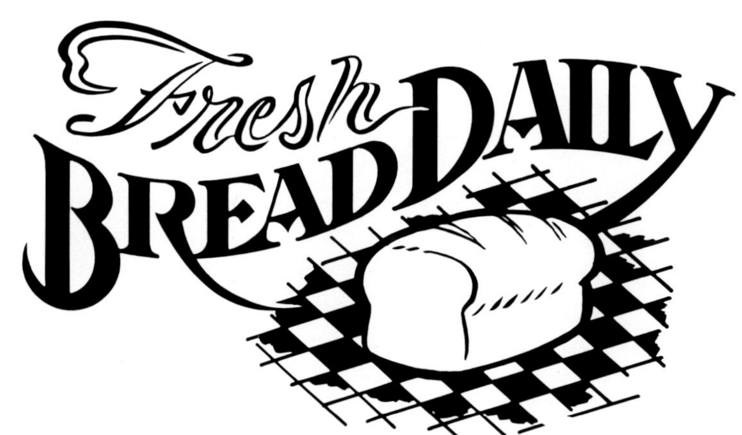

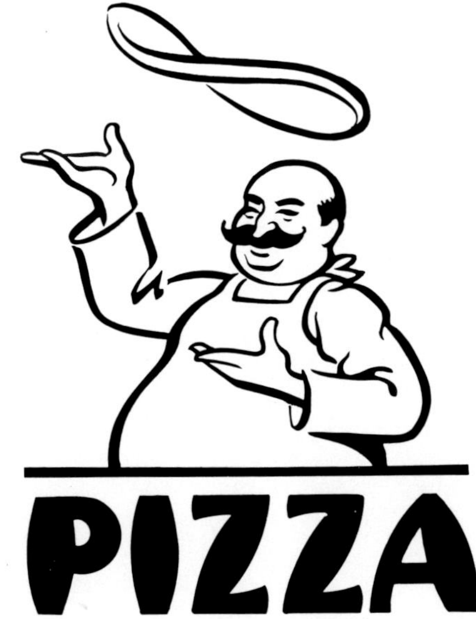

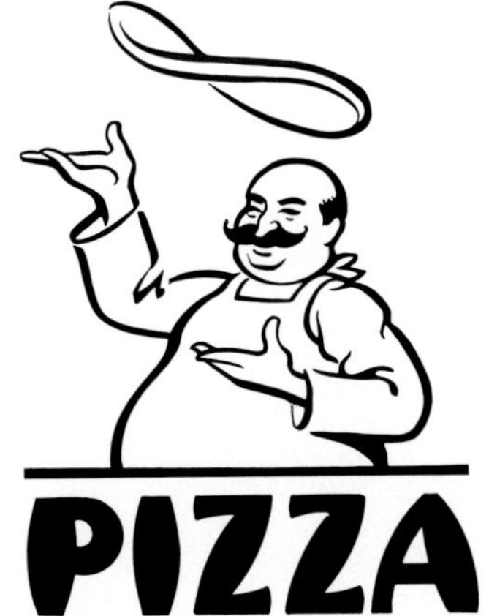

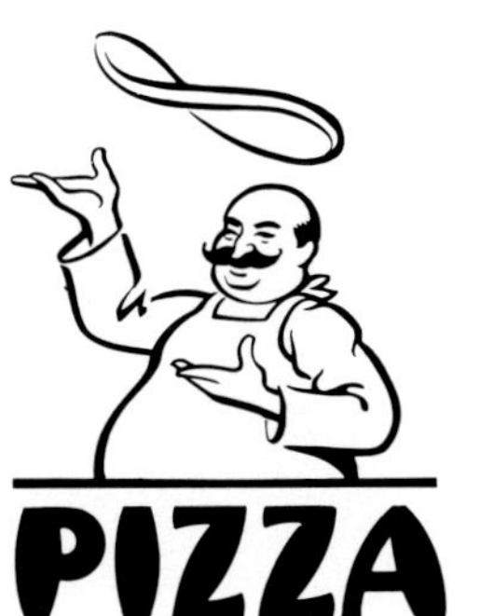

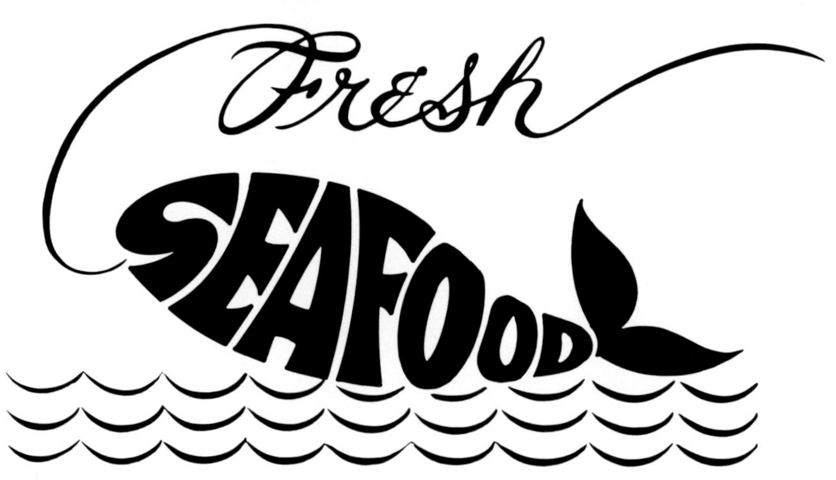
Fresh
SEAFOOD
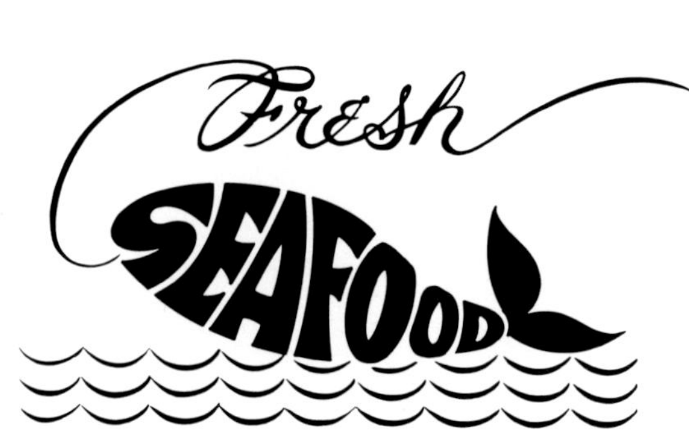
Fresh
SEAFOOD
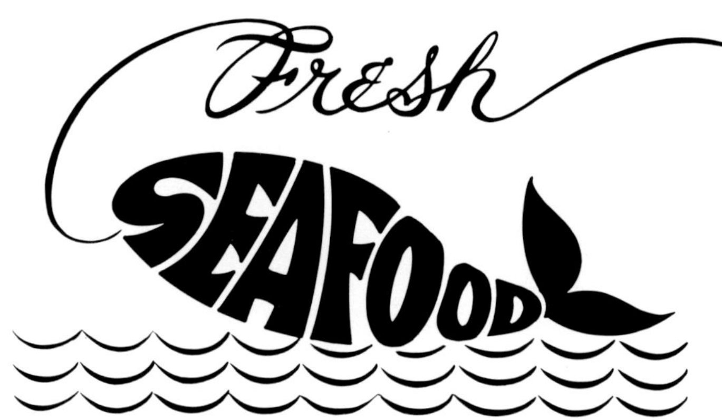
Fresh
SEAFOOD
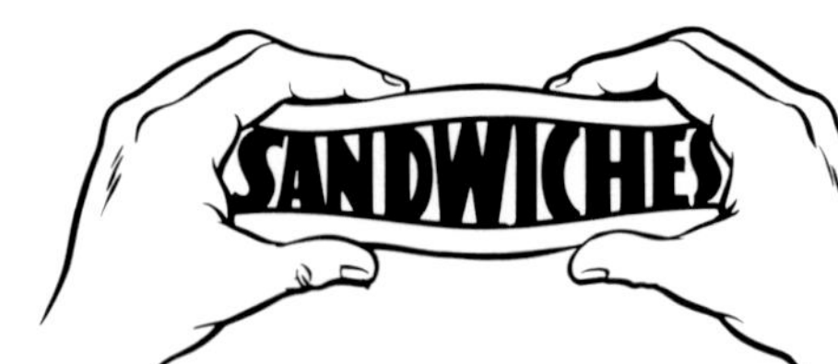
SANDWICHES
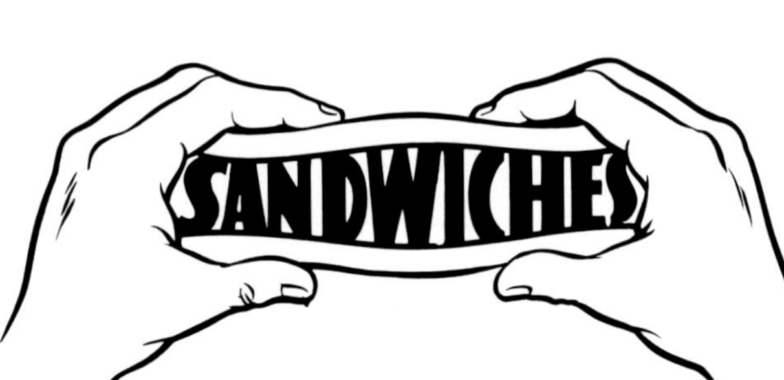
SANDWICHES
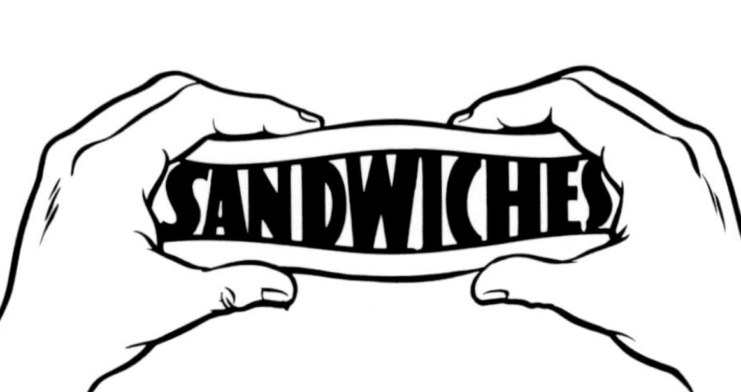
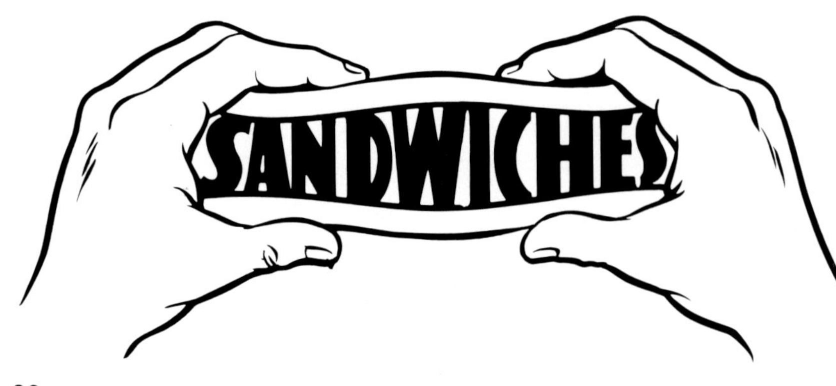
SANDWICHES
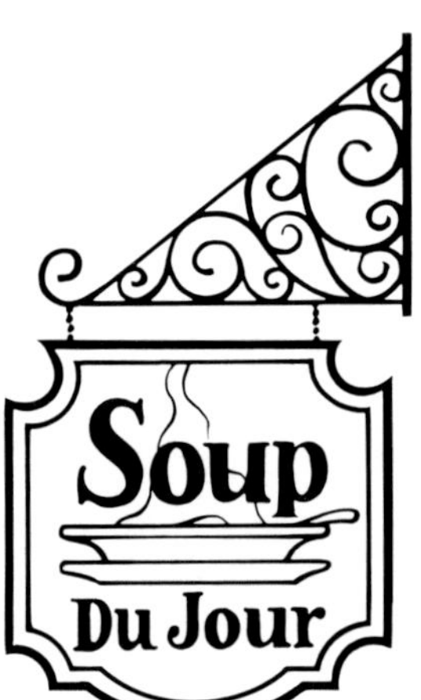
Soup
Du Jour
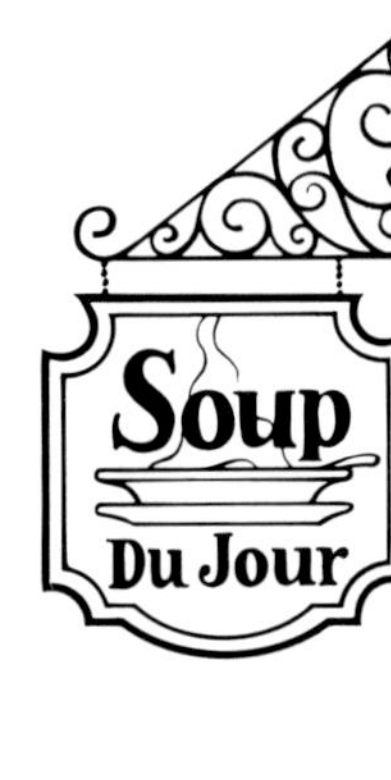
Soup
Du Jour
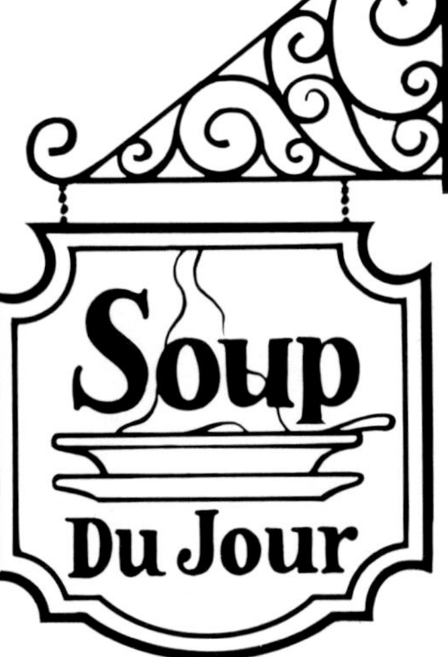
Soup
Du Jour

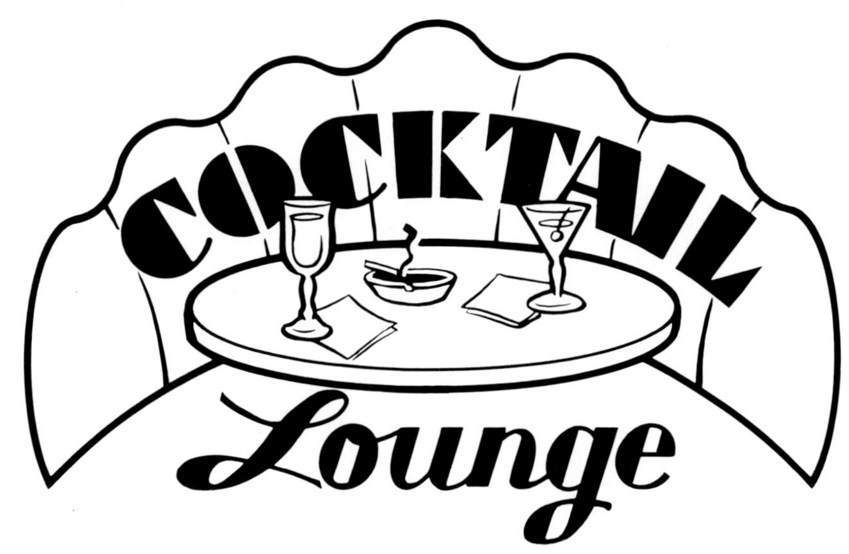

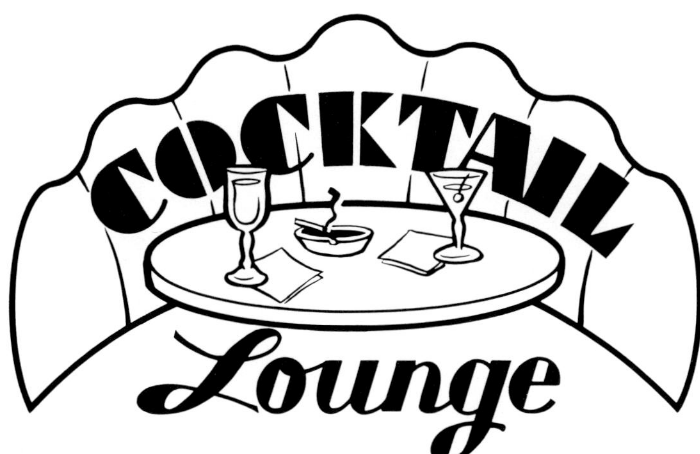

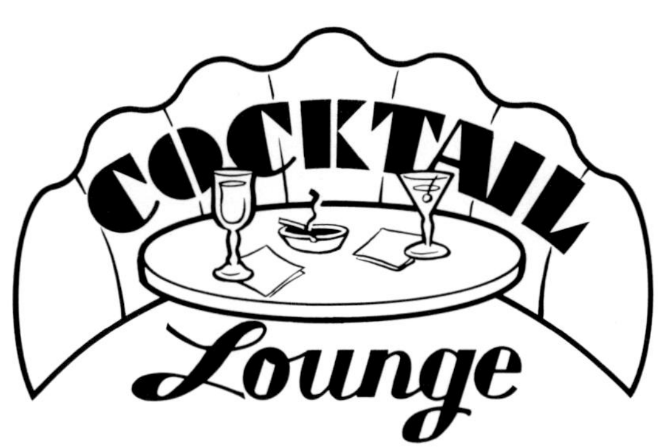

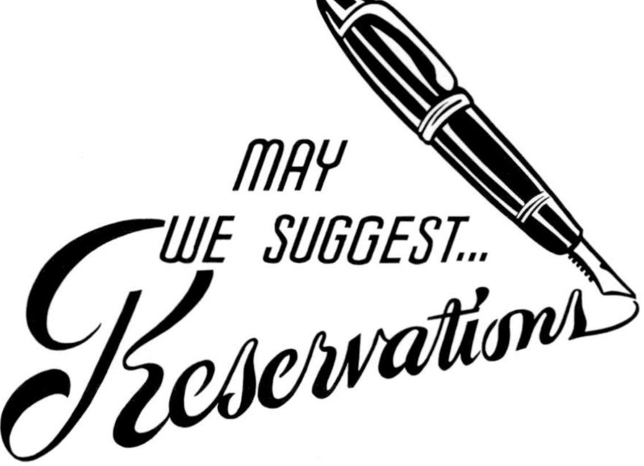

MAY
WE SUGGEST...
Reservations

MAY
WE SUGGEST...
Reservations

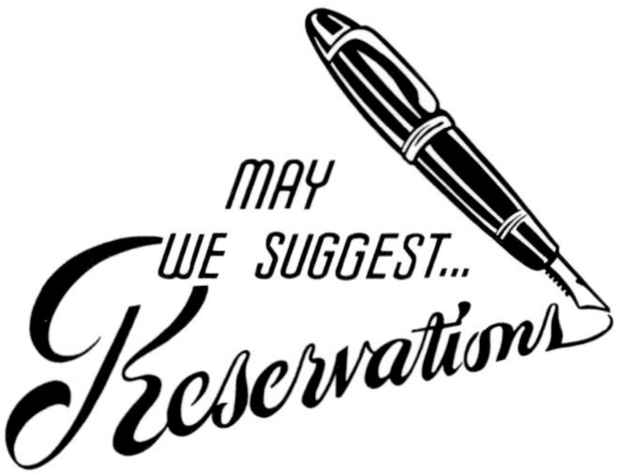

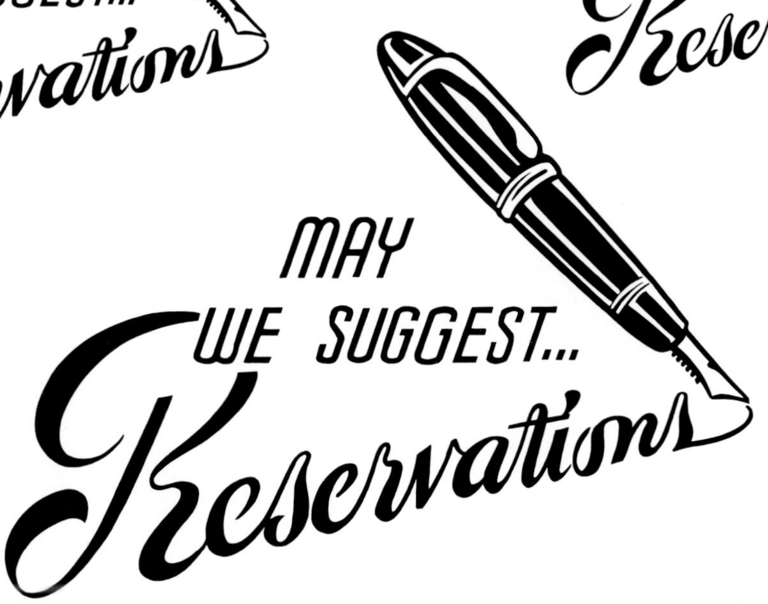

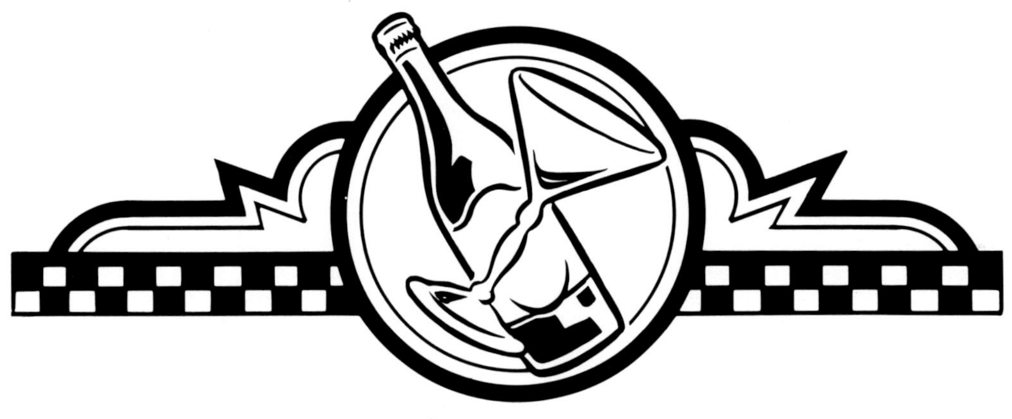

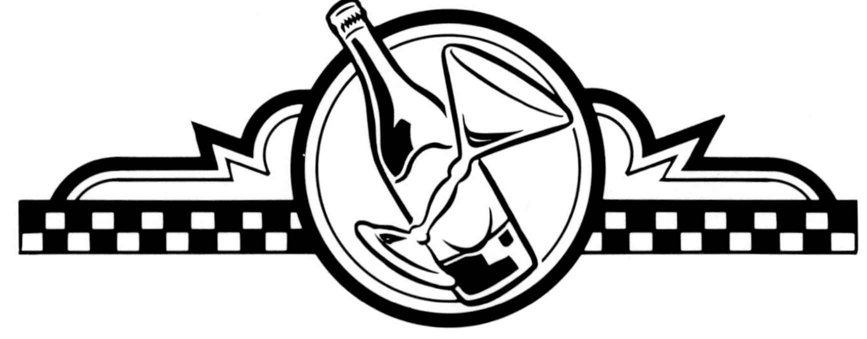

Restaurant AND Bar

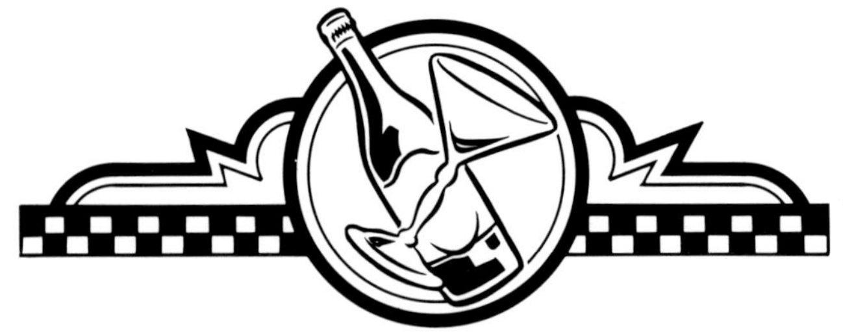

Restaurant AND Bar

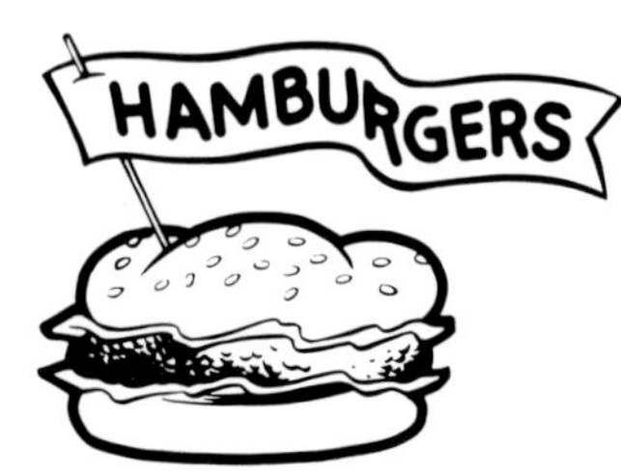

Restaurant AND Bar

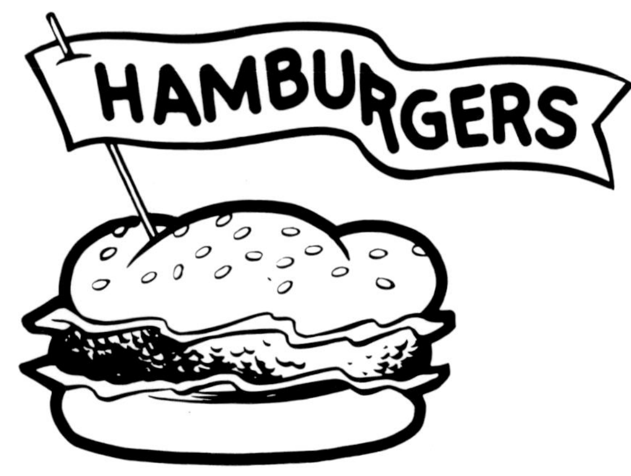

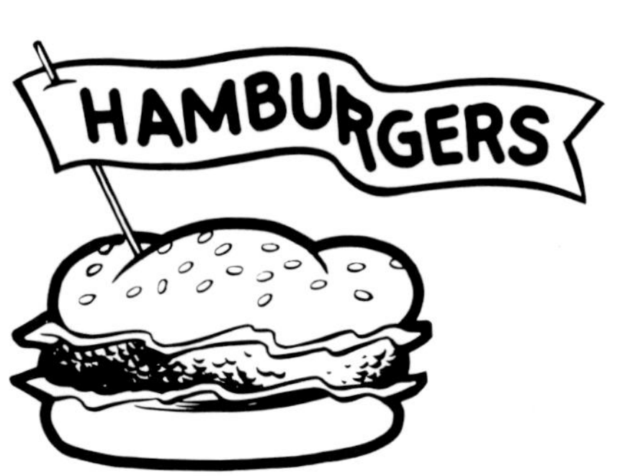

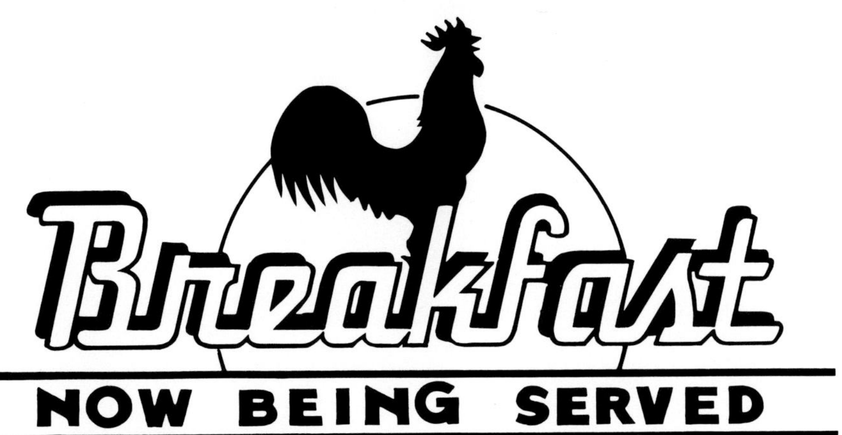
Breakfast
NOW BEING SERVED

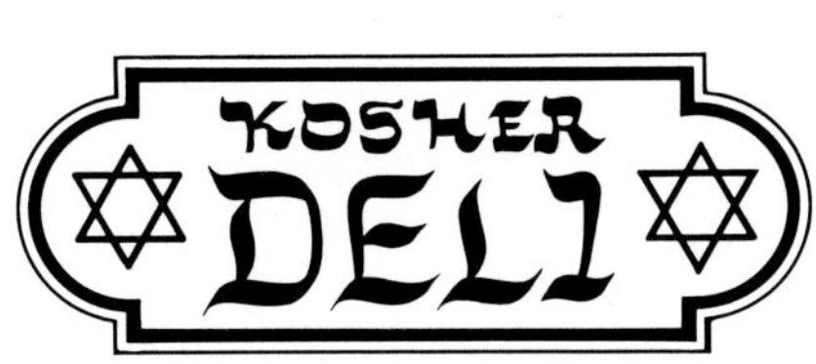
KOSHER
DELI

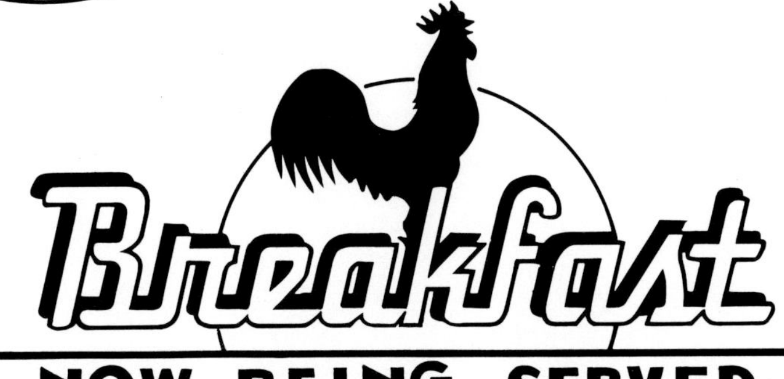
Breakfast
NOW BEING SERVED

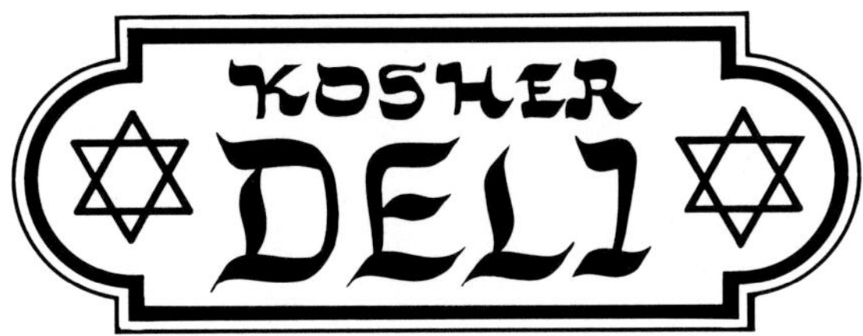
KOSHER
DELI

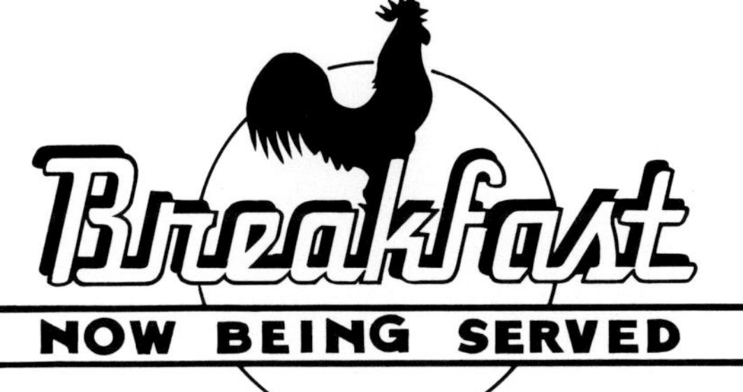
Breakfast
NOW BEING SERVED

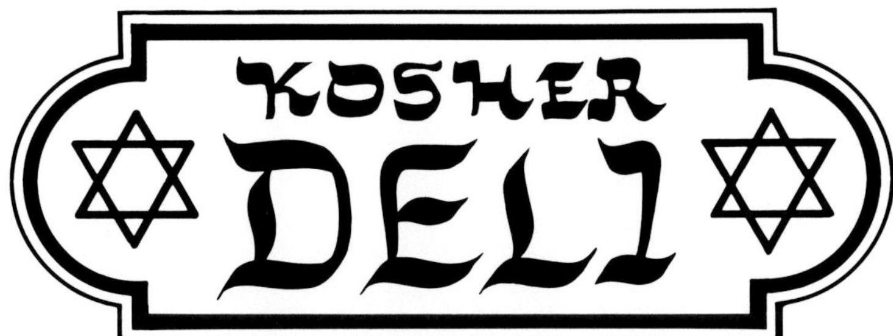
KOSHER
DELI

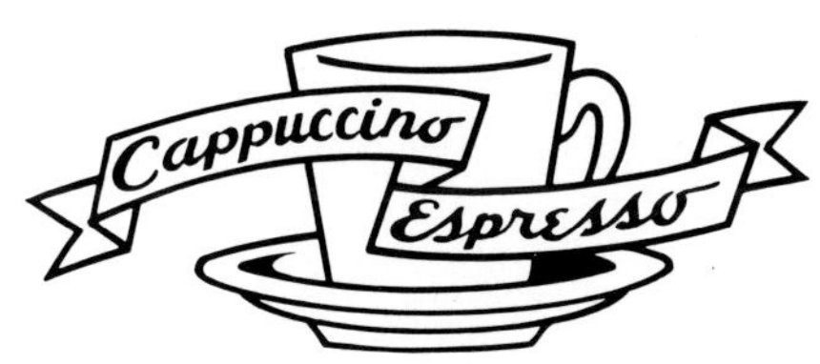
Cappuccino
Espresso

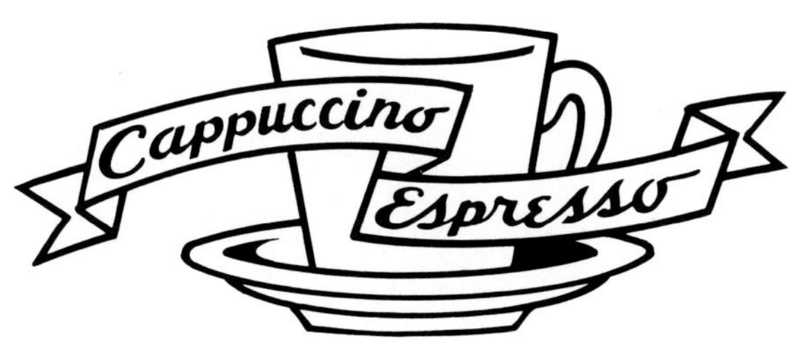
Cappuccino
Espresso

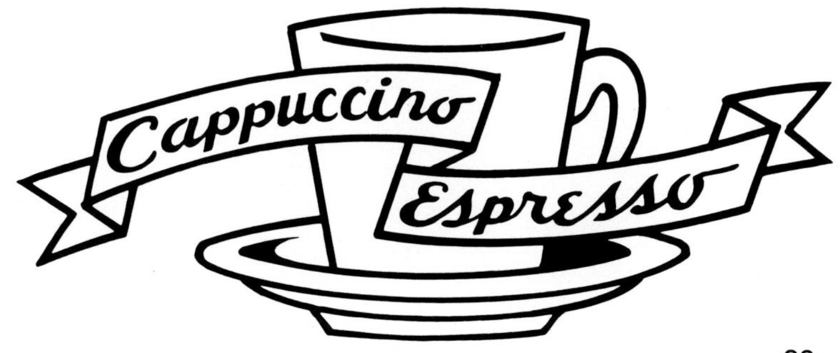
Cappuccino
Espresso

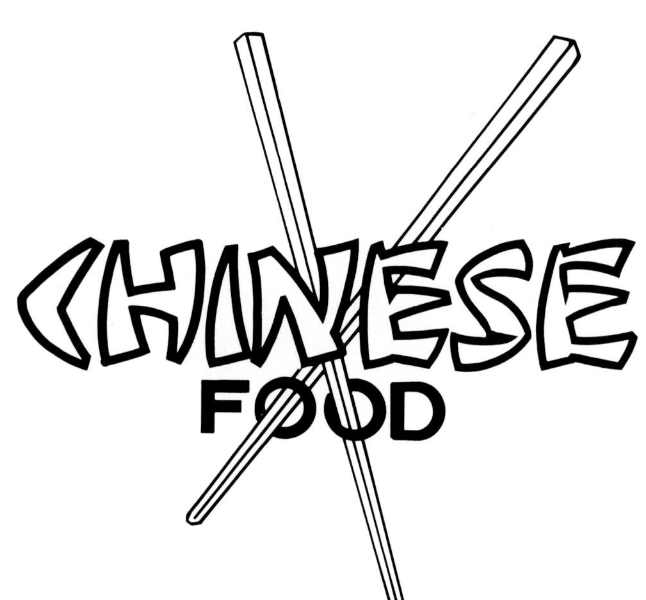
CHINESE
FOOD
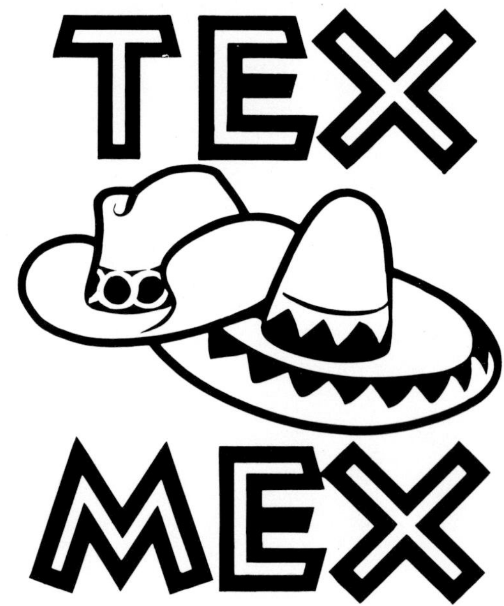
TEX
MEX
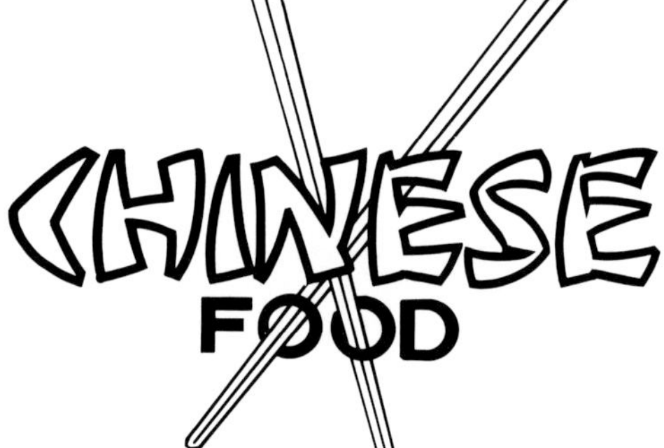
CHINESE
FOOD
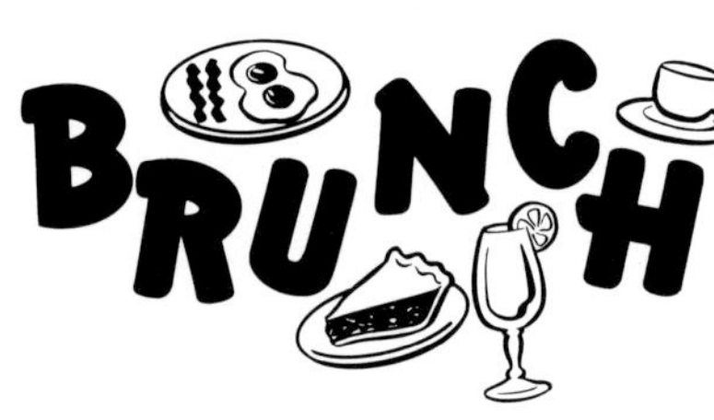
BRUNCH
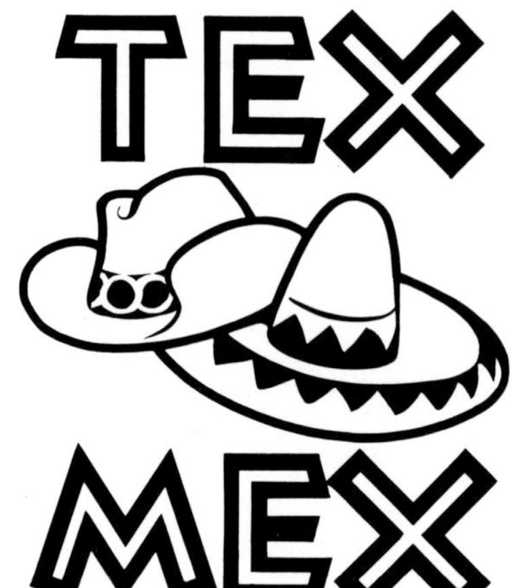
TEX
MEX
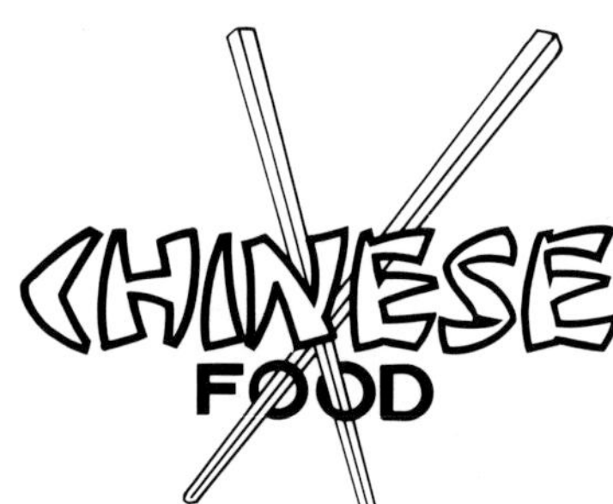
CHINESE
FOOD
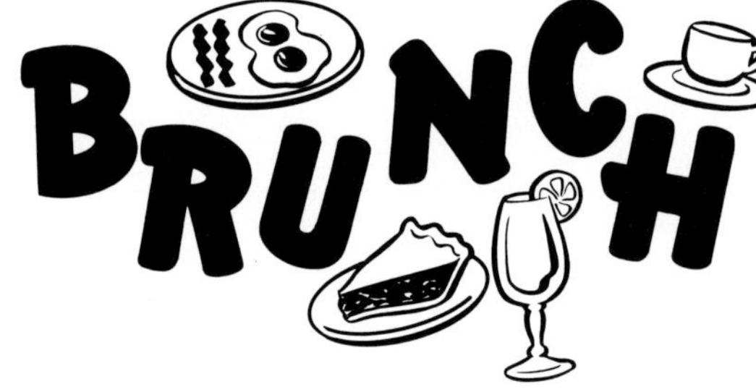
BRUNCH
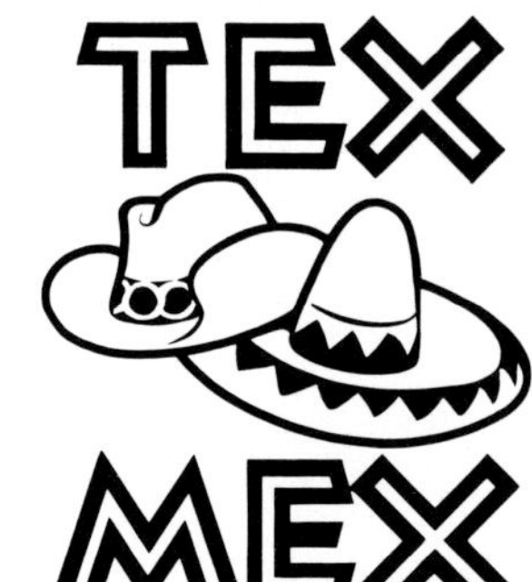
TEX
MEX
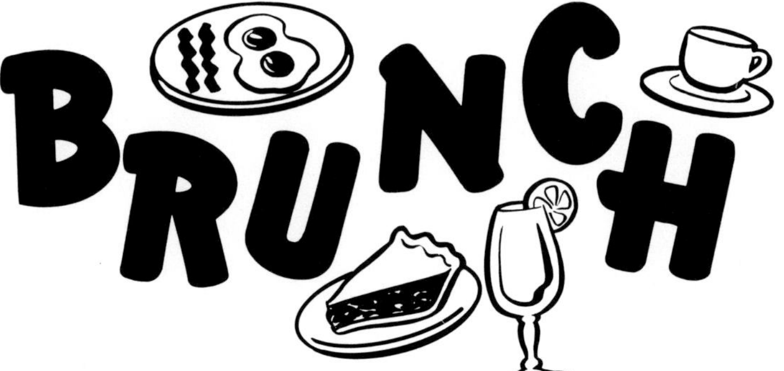
BRUNCH

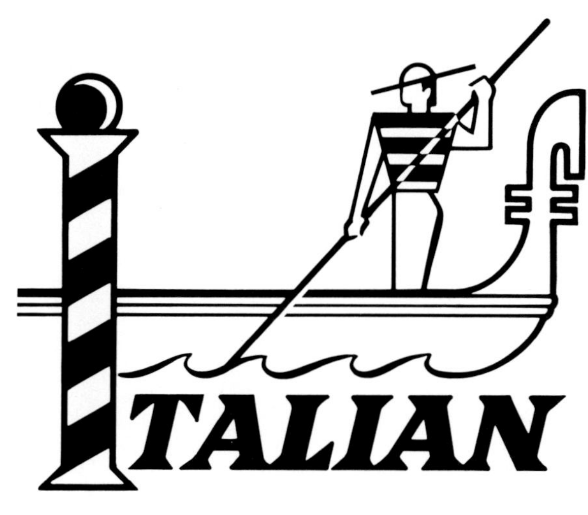
ITALIAN

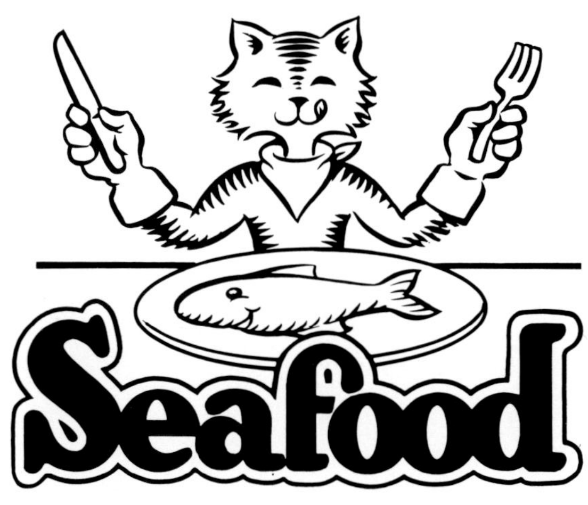
Seafood

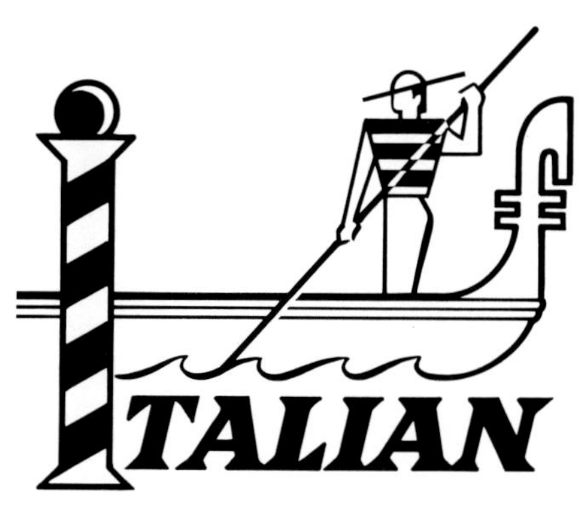
ITALIAN

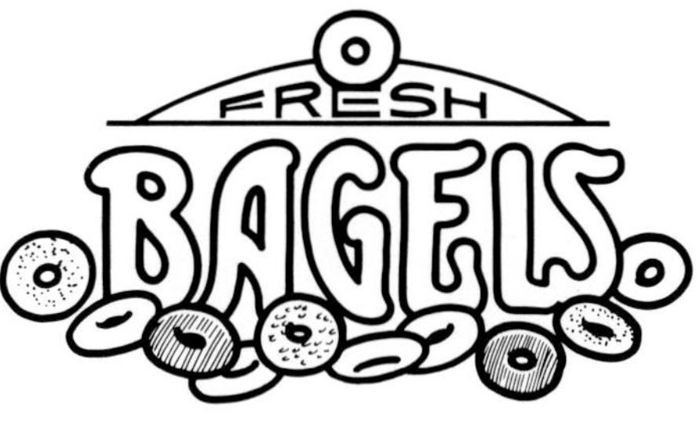
FRESH
BAGELS

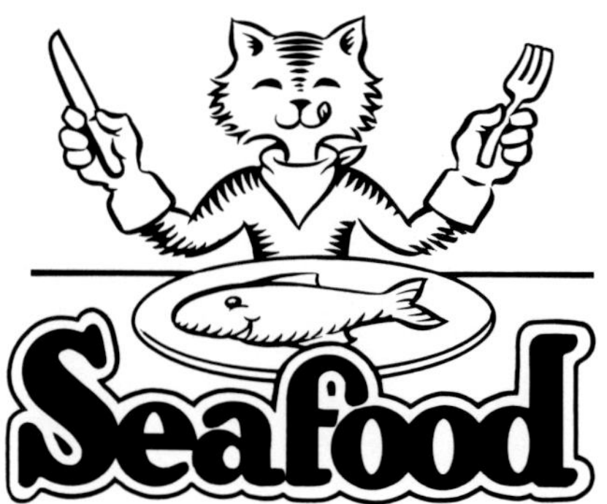
Seafood

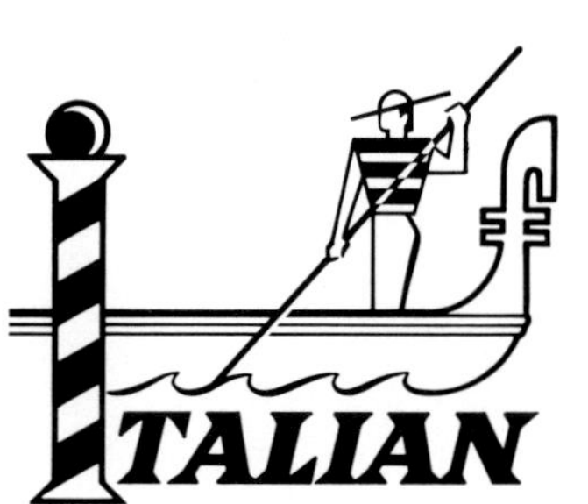
ITALIAN

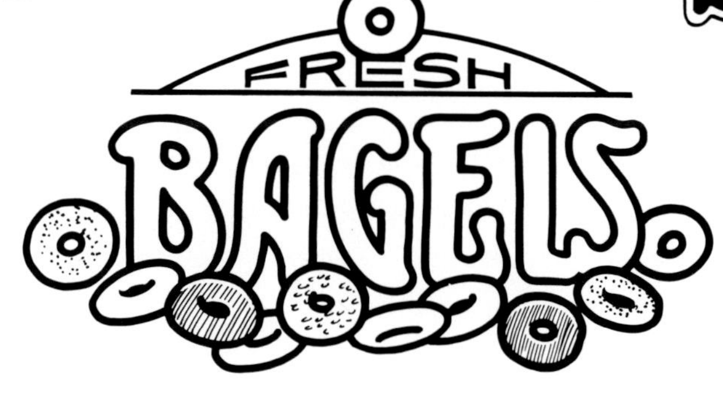
FRESH
BAGELS

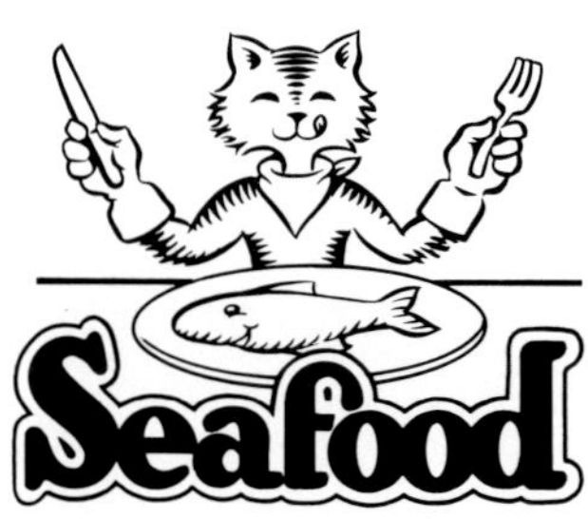
Seafood

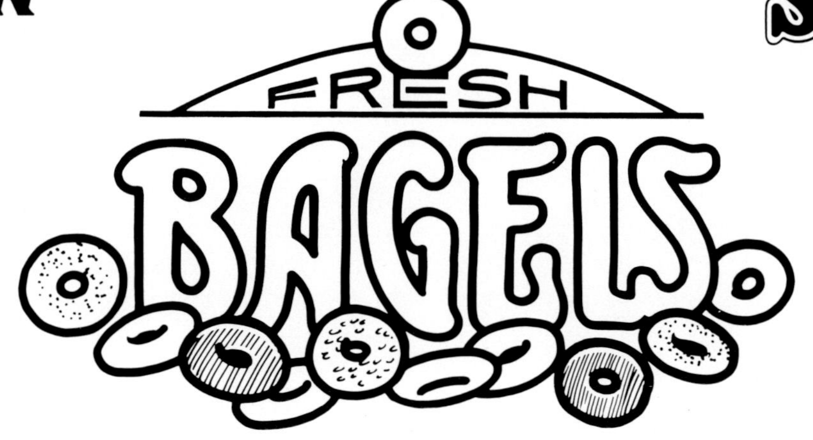
FRESH
BAGELS

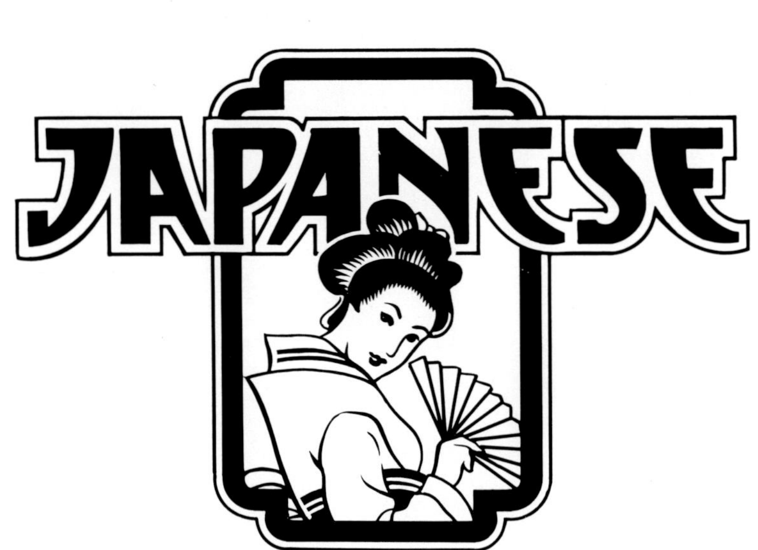
JAPANESE

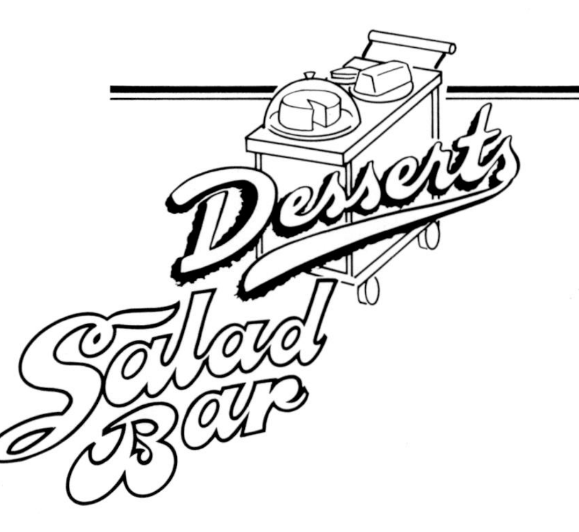
Desserts
Salad
Bar

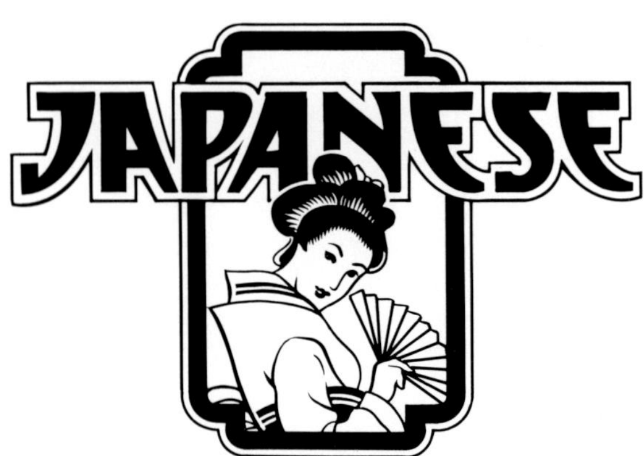
JAPANESE

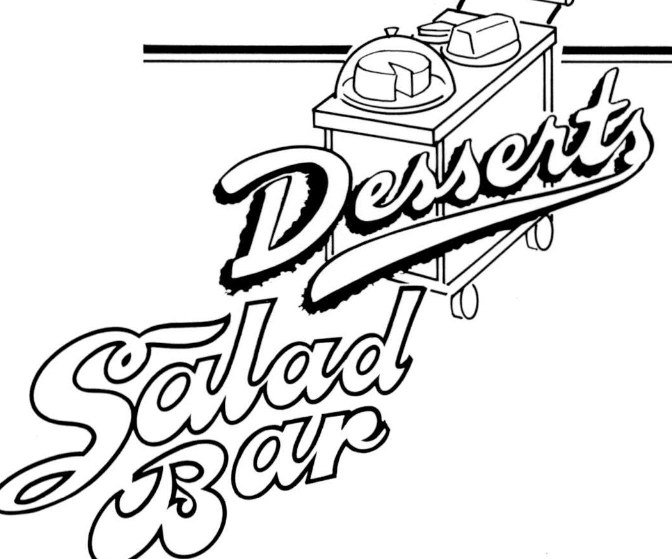
Desserts
Salad
Bar

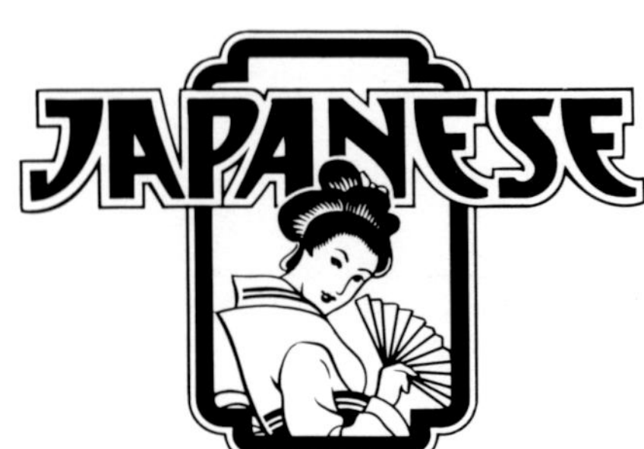
JAPANESE

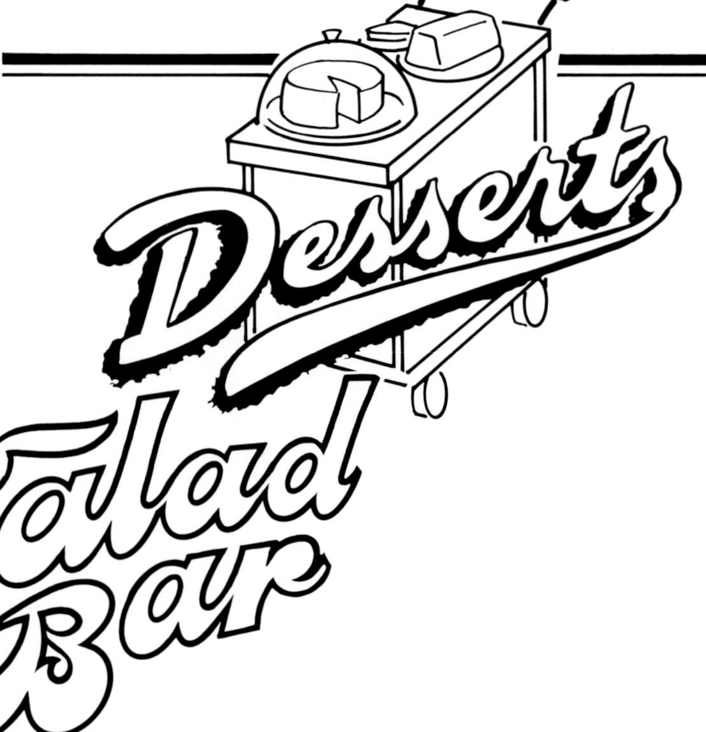
Desserts
Salad
Bar